A MISCELLANY OF MASONIC ESSAYS

ESSAYS

(1995-2012)

Other Books by Robert Lomas

The Man Who Invented the Twentieth Century

The Lost Key

Mastering Your Business Dissertation

The Secret Power of Masonic Symbols

Turning the Templar Key

The Secret Science of Masonic Initiation

Turning the Solomon Key

Turning the Hiram Key

The Invisible College

Freemasonry and the Birth of Modern Science

With Chris Knight

The Book of Hiram

Uriel's Machine

The Second Messiah

The Hiram Key

With Geoff Lancaster

Forecasting for Sales and Materials Management

Dr Robert Lomas has worked on guidance systems for cruise missiles, Fire Brigade Command and Control systems and was involved in the early development of personal computers. He currently lectures in Technological Management at Bradford University School of Management in Yorkshire in the UK. He is author, or co-author, of many best-selling books on Freemasonry and Science including *The Hiram Key*, *Turning the Hiram Key, Freemasonry and the Birth of Modern Science* and *The Man Who Invented the Twentieth Century*.

www.robertlomas.com

twitter @Dr_Robert_Lomas

A Miscellany of Masonic Essays (1995-2012)

Robert Lomas

www.robertlomas.com

First published in 2012
by Dowager Digital

This editions published 2013

By Dowager Books

ISBN-13:

978-1482042283

ISBN-10:

1482042282

Printed by Amazon CreateSpace

DOWAGER BOOKS
www.dowager.com

Dedicated to

Two Brethren who inspired many of these essays by posing questions for me to try to answer

Bro. Framz Minwalla and Bro. Tony Baker.

Foreword

As a practicing academic I have a great fondness for the essay both as a means of conveying information and as a tool to help me think through ideas that interest me. I write essays for various reasons. I write them to investigate issues, I write them for my own amusement, I write them to clarify my ideas, I write them because people ask me to comment on particular topics, I write them to send out in newsletters and I write them because I am invited to give public lectures and need to prepare the material I want to deliver.

All the essays I write end up stored somewhere in the murky recesses of my data storage system where they remain to haunt me when I stumble across them while looking for something more important. It cannot be denied that among them I have essays written about a whole range of Masonic topics which I think are interesting.

Recently one of my publishers happened to email me about a particular topic and I casually mentioned I had written something about it. What have you written? came back the reply. I promptly retrieved an essay on the topic, attached it to the email and sent it off.

Their reply came back quickly. Have you got any more of these essays?

They grow in my backup drives like mould on a damp wall, I replied.

In that case why not put together a collection of your favourites? They said.

So I delved into the bowels of my hard drive and here is the result. Each essay is a self-contained unit which poses a question and then tries to answer it.

There is no particular theme to the collection, except Freemasonry. I have included essays about the philosophy of Freemasonry, about its past, its present practice and its possible futures. Some are formally documented and referenced, some are not, some are written for the general public and assume no prior knowledge and others are written as a Freemason writing for other Masons. They span a period of seventeen years. Amongst them you find many ideas which I have later written about more fully in various books. These essays are where these ideas started life. You will also find some essays I wrote simply to clarify my own thoughts or to explain why I felt as I do about some issues.

I hope you enjoy reading them as much as I enjoyed writing them.

Robert Lomas.

Halifax. 2012

Table of Contents

Introduction – by Anthony Baker 1

Essay 1 - What is Freemasonry? 3

Essay 2 - What is a Freemason? 11

Essay 3 - Why-Freemasonry- A Catechismal Response 17

Essay 4 - The Nature of Masonic Truth 23

Essay 5 - The Quest for Masonic Illumination 29

Essay 6 - The Corporate Identity of the Perfect Lodge 37

Essay 7 - The Purposes of the Dark Silence 43

Essay 8 - The Importance of a Questioning Attitude 49

Essay 9 - Understanding and Practicing Brotherly Love 55

Essay 10 - Thoughts on a Black and White Pavement 65

Essay 11 - The Mystery of the Ashlars 71

Essay 12 - How does a Mason Progress? 79

Essay 13 – Wilmshurst - A Symbolic Summary of the Craft - the Tracing Board of the Centre 85

Essay 14 - The Influence of Freemasonry on the Life and Work of Bro, Sir Robert Moray, Soldier, Scientist, Spy, Freemason and Founder of the Royal Society. 101

Essay 15 - Why Should a Quantum Physicist Take Freemasonry Seriously? 133

Essay 16 - What Should Freemasonry Do? 157

Essay 17 - Whither or Wither Freemasonry? 165

Essay 18- Why become a Freemason?   An Appeal to the Next Generation. 173

Essay 19 - Some Questions and My Answers 179

Endnotes 187

Bibliography 189

Introduction – by Anthony Baker

It is a great pleasure to introduce this collection of Masonic essays by Robert Lomas.

Robert, himself of course, needs no introduction to the Masonic world. He is a controversial figure and he is proud of the fact. He believes passionately that English Freemasonry has lost its way and no longer understands what its prime purpose should be. In attempting to put this right he has tried, in his many books, to show his Brethren as well as interested non-Masons what Freemasonry teaches and the enormous value that it could have for the modern world.

In doing so, however, he has, in the view some of his Brethren, revealed rather too much of what they believe they should keep to themselves; and as a result he has made enemies, even within the Fraternity. Robert understands this but feels that it is a price he is willing to pay, since he is doing his best to save an Order he loves so dearly. He is unable to sit by and watch Freemasonry, which is important to him, "dumbed down" into some sort of charitable and social club. He cannot do nothing while the Order withers and dies.

In spite of the fact that there are those who find his approach undesirable, his books are hugely popular, testifying to the fact that his views find a welcome in the minds of many. He hopes to stimulate his Brethren – to rekindle their interest in the deeper meanings of the Craft. He also wishes to show the real value of the Masonic system to those who are not yet Freemasons but who would find the teachings of the Craft of great value if only they had some inkling of what those teachings actually are. Robert provides such information and, in this way, he tries to foster interest in Freemasonry and to help to increase its membership by attracting more of those with a deep and sincere interest.

Many of these essays were written as one of a group of three members of the Lodge of Living Stones (No. 4957), a group he referred to in the first chapter of his book *The Lost Key*. (Lomas, R *The Lost Key* (2011), Coronet, London, pp. 9-10). These three Brethren set a question every couple of months, to which they each wrote an answer. After their Lodge meeting they remained behind and compared and discussed their answers over a drink or two. I have to say that these discussions were some of the most stimulating and rewarding that Freemasonry has ever provided me with.

Robert is currently the Associate Members' Secretary of the Lodge of Living Stones and in this capacity he writes a letter to the Associate Members four times a year, on some aspect of the teachings of Freemasonry. He particularly enjoys being set a topic on which to write and one or two of us enjoy thinking up a title that might stretch him a little. Some of his letters are included in this collection.

He has also included two papers that he presented to the Bristol Masonic Society at my invitation. All in all I think that this collection will stimulate the thinking Freemason, who is earnestly searching for "that which is lost", and should also interest those who are not yet Freemasons but who are wondering whether to join us.

If, as you read, you find that you disagree with what he says – with his interpretation of our rituals and ceremonies, all you need to do is contact him and I am sure he will be willing to engage in discussion with you. He likes nothing more than to defend his views on subjects such as these.

A.R. Baker MA, MD, FRCS

(Master of the Lodge of Living Stones – No. 4957)

Essay 1 - What is Freemasonry?

Freemasonry is a force which can make three mature, professional men; a psychologist, a surgeon and a physicist, stand in a dark and cold car park late on a wet and foggy September evening and talk for an hour and a half about their deepest spiritual urges.

That meeting of three such Masons: a student of the human mind; a student of the human body; and a student of the workings of the world humans inhabit, prompted this essay. What is the nature of the force which can bring together such a disparate collection of individuals to share their inner most feelings?

The lodge we had earlier attended is far from a model of perfection. It is a run by fallible, elderly men, each holding different views of the world, each motivated in different ways by sincere intentions and all with totally different experiences of life. It has factions which adopt different philosophies, each with its own heroes and demons. One faction believes truth is to be found by talking, questioning and engaging in friendly argument. Another believes truth can only be found in silent contemplation. It has groups who are at peace with their inner motives, and it has groups who are deeply uncertain about what they are doing or they should do next.

This motley crew of pilgrims disagree about methods of approach; about matters of continuity; and even about the function of the meeting they have all travelled many miles in bad weather to attend. What brings them together? What entices them to put aside their many differences and work within their limited areas of communality? just one thing, their shared search for the truth about the human condition.

It is their ability to set aside differences and concentrate on shared values which represents the hope of a solution to a modern dilemma, the conflict between religion and science.

Western civilization is founded on two pillars. The scientific spirit of curiosity - the observation of the hidden mysteries of nature and science, the attitude that anything and everything may be questioned within the enforced humility of uncertainty and that all assertions should be tested - and the ethics of Christianity- the brotherhood of all men, the value of the individual and the importance of love in motivating actions. Logically there should be no conflict between these two founding principles. Science simply says, 'What will happen if I do this?' making no judgment on the morality of the action. Ethics says, 'Should I do this?' having no view on the practically of what is to be done.

But is logic enough? To follow an idea, it must first engage your heart. You must be inspired. But to reason it through, to understand and apply it you must question, analyze and doubt. Where do you seek for a source of strength and courage to persevere in this daunting search for truth? Traditionally religion provided that inspiration, while science's role was to provide the working tools to understand and share insights. But in modern society this accommodation is seriously weakened. Let me consider why.

In my view religion is based on two metaphysical concepts and one pragmatic one. The first is that there exists a personal God to whom you pray in order to influence his actions. Secondly this God had something to do with creating the universe. And thirdly the practical consequence is that the words of this God are intended to guide you in your morals.

Religion demands a certainty of belief which directly conflicts with science, which deals only with questions which can be put into a form which can be tested by experiment. Impartial observations decide the truth of a scientific assertion. Religion deals with questions outside this category such 'would it be right to do this thing?'

The conflict between religion and science arises when the ethical and inspirational qualities of religion are claimed as a monopoly by those who express an absolute faith in the metaphysical aspects. No scientist can do this. I do not believe it is possible for religious theology to discover a set of metaphysical ideas which can be guaranteed not to get into conflict with the ever advancing and always changing ideas of science as it continues to probe the unknown. But this conflict only occurs in the class of questions concerning 'What happens if I do this?' or 'Does this particular entity exist and how does it interact with me?'

Let me give an example. The universe is extremely large. Lie on your back on a clear night in a field well away from the city lights and you cannot fail to be impressed with the number and beauty of the stars. Then consider that what you are seeing is merely the local stars of our own galaxy. There are more galaxies in creation than stars in our galaxy, each galaxy contains hundreds of millions of stars and there are billions of other galaxies. Some are so far away that their light takes billions of years to reach us. Our sun is but a tiny particle whirling among a hundred thousand million other suns in our own Milky Way.

Now think about the wondrous brotherhood of the life forms in our fragile biosphere. Every single one of the millions of species of life which exists, or has existed in our planet's past, is made up of an immortal mix of carbon, hydrogen and oxygen atoms, stitched together by the complex codes of DNA which make up the great plan of life. Man is a late-arrival in this vast evolving drama and it seems unlikely that the whole four billion year enterprise was set motion just to allow him to become Lord of Creation, or that it will end with him.

The atoms from which the stars, the Earth, the human race and my socks are all created appear to follow immutable laws. Nothing can escape these laws: stars become novas because of them: tidal waves rise up and swamp the land because of them: and my brain is able to think because of them.

It is a great adventure to imagine the universe beyond the limited reach of man. Think of the great majority of beautiful and strange places which we see through our telescopes. They have never known the footfall of a human. Once you have considered this vast panorama of mystery and wonder, turn back and look at the transient patterns of matter which make up the human race. Life is part of a universal mystery of enormous depth. It is brief dance of transient coupling by promiscuous, yet immortal, particles of matter. Truly I can bring nothing into this life and surely take nothing from it? For I cannot even own, let along control, the atoms which make up my body. As my cells grow, mature and die they are replaced by new cells, containing different atoms. So what am I? I am nothing more than a temporary and shimmering pattern of atoms which choose for a brief moment to stay with each other before moving on to dance with new partners. The carbon, which is such an important binding agent in my DNA, is nothing more than the waste matter of an ancient hydrogen furnace which exploded into a super nova billions of years ago. Romantically we are formed from star-dust. Prosaically we are made of atomic waste. Yet religion would have me accept unconditionally that such preposterous creatures are the sole preoccupation of the majesty of the Cosmos.

Ultimately a scientific view of creation ends in awe and mystery, in the contemplation of the vast expanses of the Universe, or in the nature of the sub-atomic zoo which blossoms when we try to shake the quarks out of our nuclei. At each end of the scale science melds into an uncertainty which is deep and impressive. But it is hard to accept that this has all been simply arranged for a personal God to preside over man's struggle with good and evil.

Now if a person's ethical and moral views are based in religion these insights of science can pose enormous problems. If morality is based only on the instructions of personal God and you begin to doubt that such a limited and parochial God could be responsible for the vast scope of creation you begin to entertain doubts about the value of the ethical teaching which he is said to promote. That is where Freemasonry offers a way forward.

To become a Freemason you only need to express a belief in the existence of an order at the centre of creation. This is metaphorically expressed as a belief in Supreme Being, the nature of which is not questioned but left to your own conscience. Masonry leaves you free, to join with me and believe in the immutable, but statistically uncertain laws, which govern the interactions of atoms without forcing us to ascribe human characteristics onto the Great Architect of the Universe. Or if you prefer you can adopt any of the conventional religious theologies which appeal to you. Jew, Muslim, Christian, Hindu or Buddist, as long as you accept that there is some sort of Supreme force for order in the universe you are welcome. As we will never discuss religion in a lodge, then we will never trespass on each other's sincerely accepted beliefs.

Here is the truth in the statement that Freemasonry is peculiar system of morality. It is peculiar, in the sense of being singular and unique, in that it teaches ethics without insisting on the need to accept any particular metaphysical concept. But this alone does not answer my earlier question "What is the nature of the force which can bring together such a disparate collection of individuals to share their inner most feelings?".

The psychologist, the surgeon and the physicist all agreed that the experience of the lodge meeting and the participation in working the ritual with individuals who shared a hunger for spiritual truth created something which was bigger than their individual egos. But admitting the imperfections of the reality of the lodge, how does the Craft achieve this magic? It does it in three ways.

Firstly it teaches a new language based on metaphor and symbolism to help you share and learn. The Craft wisely forbids the preaching of religion or politics within the lodge. So individuals of widely differing philosophies learn a common mode of speech, which they are free to adapt to their own understanding of life. The details of my conception of the Great Architect may well seen cold, distant and impersonal to a follower of the Christian Master, but by using the symbolic language of Masonry I can share my sense of awe and wonder without either of us offending the other's devoutly held views.

Secondly it teaches that at the centre of human consciousness, as represented by the Masonic model of the Perfect Lodge, there is a unique awareness that each individual is part of something much greater than himself. This light at the centre can be reached by any Mason who is properly prepared, by the disciplines of Masonic ritual and who has learned the universal language of Masonic symbolism. To my scientist's mind it offers confirmation that I am indeed just a temporary conglomeration of immortal atoms which have been the fuel source of stars, the bones of dinosaurs and the trunks of majestic trees. And when I reach down into the dark centre of my consciousness, into the tomb of my individual ego I will find that light which at first is only darkness visible and experience the reality of the connections my basic quarks share with the rest of creation.

And finally Masonry provides inspiration. The Craft teaches that the grave is a cold and lonely place. But when I am lowered into the stygian darkness of the secret chamber of my inner consciousness, if I have the support of a lodge, I will be hauled back to reality. The cable tow about my waist relieves my fear that I might become lost in the darkness of madness. This knowledge of the centre, of the connectedness of all the cosmos is a wonderful source of inspiration, and it is entirely free of the metaphysical baggage which encumbers much of the historical teaching of religions.

If Western civilization is looking for a way to reconcile the conflict between its two foundation pillars, the curious uncertainty of science, and the ethical and inspirational tradition of Christianity, then the model which Bro Wilmshurst created in the Lodge of Living Stones has much to commend it.

And finally to answer the question, "What is Freemasonry?".

An inspired spiritual path which is broad and tolerant enough to encompass the vigorous curiosity of science and the benevolent brotherly love of Christian ethics. And it is the duty of all brethren to preserve and promote this message of hope for the future.

Essay 2 - What is a Freemason?

The answer to this question depends on your point of view and those possible points of view split into four major types.

These are:

1. People who are only vaguely aware of Freemasonry.

2. People who are fans of conspiracy and thriller literature.

3. People who are anti-Masons

4. And finally Masons themselves.

A survey of public attitudes to Freemasonry, (sample size 1034) carried out by a colleague at Bradford University, found that about 30% of the population believe the only purpose for becoming a Freemason is to further your personal interests at the expense of non-Masons. Most of the people holding this view also reported they had little knowledge of Freemasonry beyond what they had read in the media. People who had experience of Masonry by and large saw it as a system of personal, charitable and spiritual development. The phrase 'making good men better' occurred quite often in their responses.

This data suggests that groups 1 and 3 can be grouped together, as people without any knowledge of the Craft who rely on the media for their image of it and often see that image as anti-Masonic.

But even within Freemasonry there are differences in what a Freemason is thought to be. Just over 10% of the Masons who responded to this survey thought that their main purpose in becoming part the Craft was charity and fund-raising (they felt Freemasonry was a sort of Round Table which dressed up in pinnies when it met). A slightly larger group larger group saw the Craft as a system for preserving tradition and ritual as a means of teaching an individual about himself.

The view of group 2 is that Freemasons are the custodians of deep hidden secrets about the true origins and destiny of mankind. About two thirds of this group view Masons as benign guardians of this tradition, while the other third see them as evil, manipulative members of a secret Order of Illuminati who are covertly organizing wars and coups in order to bring about a New World Order which they will control.

The most popular single words used by Masons to describe the Craft were brotherhood, fraternity and morality. Those without personal experience of Freemasonry favoured the words secretive, evil and elitist.

Clearly these viewpoints are not just different they are in complete opposition to each other.

If we leave the suspicions of the Dan Brown fans, and accept that we are not being manipulated by Grand Lodge, and its familiar creature Lodge QC, into supporting an attempt to rule the world by stealth then the question resolves to a bipolar issue. A Freemason is either an individual who is seeking to understand and develop their personal nature or is a self-seeking, avaricious and greedy individual who sets out to join a secret society which aims to help its members succeed, at the expense of non-Masons.

Whilst accepting that the poor handling of media curiosity makes it easy to promote the latter attitude, it is not an accurate description of the majority of Freemasons I have met. So why has such a poor media perception of Freemasons arisen? The reasons are historical and complex.

Prior to the First World War Freemasonry was far more public, its members were proud to admit membership and public processions of Masons, dressed in full regalia, were common. The local Masons were seen as pillars of their local society and acceptance by the lodge was a mark of social distinction, at least in class-conscious England.

The end of the Great War saw an enormous influx of men joining the Craft who were seeking to replace the camaraderie they had experienced during the horrific fighting in the killing fields of France and Freemasonry could offer that. Few of these veterans ever discussed their experiences with their wives, or family, but they could talk openly with fellow old soldiers in the 'smoking rooms' of their lodges. The culture of the new lodges tended to reflect the 'Officers and other ranks' society which had been such a part of the military position during the Great War. Although the teaching and ritual of Freemasonry is highly democratic, the intricate and opaque honours system in England, with its visible rewards in the form of bigger and bigger pinnies, fed this perception. So some hundred years ago English Freemasonry lost sight of the fact that its ritual teaches that Freemasons are equal and brothers, The concept of a Masonic Officer Class, chosen by right of birth and wealth, arose within the new influx of ex-military brethren who had been conditioned by years of hardship not to question the edicts of rulers and betters. A massive officer structure grew up, tightly controlled by the new 'generals of the Craft' and a complete military command structure for passing down orders from on high began to grow. But the system was still open for all to join and it was still a matter of pride to become even a foot soldier in the structure of Freemasonry between the two world wars. It allowed the condescending aristocracy to parade their virtues of charity and goodwill before the admiring gaze of the tradesmen and skilled working men who made up the subordinate ranks and so all were content.

The Second World War made an even greater impact on the public image which Freemasons choose to project. A frightening change was triggered by the open hostility to Freemasonry which arose in Nazi Germany and Communist Russia. Both Hitler and Stalin imprisoned and murdered vast numbers of Freemasons, simply for being Freemasons. Hitler accepted the view that Freemasons were Jewish fellow-travellers who were evil, manipulative members of a secret Jewish Order who were actively working to bring down the Third Reich. Hitler thought they were trying to establish a Jewish World Order which they would control and use to enslave the noble Aryan Race of Eugenically purified Nazis he envisaged. Almost 300,000 Freemasons died alongside Jews, Gypsies and other assorted "Un-Aryan-subhumans" in the death camps of the Holocaust.

Hitler was certainly superstitious and he may well have genuinely believed in the Illuminati theory. But the practical outcome was that the Nazi's active opposition to Freemasonry, in the form of closing down Temples, banning meetings, burning ritual books and arresting brethren helped bolster the idea that there was something sinister and threatening about Freemasonry.

The Library of the University of Poznan possesses a large collection of Masonic books amounting to some 80,000 volumes. This was originally put together during World War II when Heinrich Himmler's SS, under the Nazi regime in Germany, confiscated the libraries of all the Masonic lodges in Germany, and stored their books in Poland. After the war this collection remained in Poland, and only since the fall of the communist regime has its existence been known or it been given any publicity. It is the largest Masonic collection in continental Europe. It also contains material from some English lodges as the Nazi invaders of Jersey closed down the Channel Island lodges, stole their books and forbade their brethren to meet.

The end of the Second World War created another influx of ex-military initiates who both fitted into the rank structure unquestioningly and accepted what ever honours they might be given, as the price for having a 'Masonic Career'. But they now were most less likely to admit their membership in public as they knew in the event of a Communist takeover they could be first up against the wall. But this second influx of ex-servicemen, used to accepting orders without question, added to the loss of touch with reality which still pervades UGLE and it never questioned the wisdom of its growing attitude of unnecessary and unproductive secrecy.

As the trained subservient servicemen of the two wars have died out they have been replaced by different types of men. Once more these can be grouped into three categories.

1. Those join who Freemasonry for what it can do for them. They may be attracted by the networking opportunities which Freemasonry can offer. The architect John Poulson, jailed for corruption in 1974, is perhaps the most notorious. It is a sad fact that his spirit lives in some quarters, as the recent draft report which the Charity Commissioners published into their investigations into the misuse of charitable donations within a badly run Provincial Grand Lodge shows. The opaque and self-serving nature of the Masonic honours system and the conflict of interest generated by the unbridled power of "rulers" of the Craft to appoint the members of their own vetting committees has contributed to this problem. It needs to be solved if the Craft is to attract more of the type of Initiates it needs to survive.

2. Those who join Freemasonry for the friendship, conviviality and dinning opportunities. These members of, what I like to call, the 'Belly Club' all seem to enjoy the ritual but would not be attracted to an Order if it did not also provide social opportunities. These are more often older individuals, who value the friendship a lodge can provide, rather than young professionals

3. The final group are those who have come to think that Freemasonry might be able to offer an answer to many of the problems of existence and can do so in a way which is tolerant and non-denominational. They are the seed-corn of Masonry's future.

The third group are the people for whom Freemasonry evolved. They are first prepared to become a Mason in their heart. They are aware that they have questions for which there are no easy answers. But the rich mix of ritual, myth and symbolism that the

Craft provides, helps them first to understand their emotions, then encourages them to expand their intellects and finally helps them to confront the most important question of existence. What happens when I die?

The demise and decline of main-stream religion in the UK has occurred because of its lack of relevance to the transcendental concerns of spiritually-aware, but well-educated individuals. People who use scientific thinking in their professions do not accept a superstitious threat and reward system as a way to organize their busy lives. But they still hunger for spiritual teaching.

Freemasonry, at its best, can offer a route for these seekers to find answers and it is the duty of the present custodians of the path keep its entrance signposted in a way which is attractive and visible to modern people. The control freakery and class ridden honours system which has grown up during a century of war is no longer an appropriate way to manage the type of modern Freemason who will carry the Craft into the 21st Century. So what is a Freemason? - A seeker after spiritual knowledge who should be nurtured and encouraged into our Fellowship.

Essay 3 - Why-Freemasonry- A Catechismal Response

Freemasonry couches much of its traditional teaching in the form of catechisms. Let me give some examples.

Q- Why were you made a Mason?

A -For the sake of obtaining the Secrets of Masonry, and to be brought from darkness into light.

Q- Have Masons Secrets?

A - They have many invaluable ones.

Q -Where do they keep them?

A- In their Hearts.

(Taken from a Catechismal Lecture of the First Degree)

To take the words why and Freemasonry as a verbal, un-punctuated question leaves scope for a wide range of responses, and the framing of the question offers an opportunity for different and revealing insights. One obvious way to frame it would be 'Why Freemasonry?' but this form also has an obvious answer which I have stated above. To repeat, it is to obtain the secrets of Masonry and to be brought from darkness to light.

Punctuating the words as 'Why Freemasonry!' has a sense of the Eureka about it, but turns it into a joyous exhortation, not a question.

A liberal sprinkling of interrogatives Why? Freemasonry? (delivered with a continuously rising emphasis), may well capture the amazement of outsiders at our overwhelming urge to roll-up our trouser legs and hold hands in a funny way but the second question mark puts a value judgment on Freemasonry which implies an incredulity that anybody should want to get involved with it. So rejecting the obvious, restraining the ejaculation of joy and refusing to judge Freemasonry as a refuge for the terminally credulous leaves me with only one option.

When I first heard the question I played with it in the dark recesses of my mind and visualized a context for the words. Stanzas from an imaginary Masonic catechism marched across the stage of my imagination and led me to a paradoxical confusion of question and answer which I have reconstructed so that I can comment on it. Join me for a moment of existentialist madness.

Q- What is Freemasonry?

A- A peculiar system of morality, veiled in allegory, and illustrated by symbols.

Q.- Where were you made a Mason?

A- In the body of a Lodge, just, perfect, and regular.

Q. -You choose of your own freewill and accord to become a Mason?

A. - I did.

Q. - Why did you become a Mason?

A. - To answer a question which troubled me?

Q. - What was that question?

A. - Why?

Q. - And the answer?

A. - Freemasonry.

To a scientist the question 'why?' has the allure of the forbidden. It has the taint of a naughty rude word said to shock. It carries the power of Kenneth Tynan saying FUCK on national television.

Not since the heyday of Aristotelian School-men, sitting at the High Tables of our ancient universities, talking of the nature of causes as they passed the port, has the question of 'why does something exist?' been a respectable subject for physicists. In those innocent days Aristotle took the view that there were four causes.

The first was a material cause. He gave the example of a cause as the material out of which a thing comes into being and which remains present in it. He gave the example of bronze in the case of a statue, or silver in the case of a cup as their material causes. This first cause consists of the material which makes up the object.

His second cause was the form or pattern of an object, which he describes as that essence or definition which creates it. He gives as an example an octave, which is defined as a doubling of frequency, or an integer, which is defined as a whole number. This second cause is the shape, or concept, which governs the disposition of the material of the object.

His third cause was the initiating source of change which brought an object into existence. He gives as an example the concept that the father is the cause of his child. This third cause is the initiating force which brings the object into being,

But his fourth cause, the speculation of which is forbidden even to consenting scientists in private, is the cause which he said, defines the purpose of the object. He gives as an example the cause of a man's going for a walk. 'Why,' someone asks, 'is he going for a walk?' 'For the good of his health,' we reply, and when we say this we have given a reason for his doing so.

As a student of science I studied materials and their natures. I studied the mechanisms by which atoms bind themselves together. I looked at the vast structures they could form as the mysterious forces of quantum energy drew them together. I looked at how they change when heated, cooled, compressed, expanded, accelerated or restrained. But the question of why does this exist is not a question the philosophy of science equipped me to approach.

I can ask: What is the Universe?

I can ask: What shapes and patterns do the objects in the Universe take up.

I can ask: How did the Universe, begin and how will it end?

But I cannot ask: Why does the Universe exist? It is not a question which my scientific training can help me with. I have no tools of analysis and no theories of a fourth cause to draw upon.

Isaac Newton understood the hunger this question creates within the human spirit but refused to face up to it. He hid behind a meaningless religious statement that passed the buck to his personal God, saying 'Gravity explains the motions of the planets, but it cannot explain who set the planets in motion. God governs all things and knows all that is or can be done'. That is not a satisfactory answer to the question 'Why?'

As humans we have a need to understand our world and our place within it. If we do not know the truth we make up stories. The stories offer us hope and give us rules of conduct. They can be real, they can be romantic or they can be simply weird. The story of the evolution of matter, from primeval hydrogen to the complexity of uranium, is a great swirling and stirring story, and it happens to be true. The ancient Egyptians did not know this story so they substituted the idea that a great god masturbated all matter into existence in a moment of divine self-pleasuring. The theoretical underpinning of their explanation does not bear too much scrutiny and it still does not answer the question Why? To say, the Universe was created because an ancient god fancied a quick wank seems to lack any high moral purpose and to suggest that the pleasures of the flesh are all that matter. Perhaps there is no fourth cause, perhaps science is right to forbid the discussion of 'Why' in its meetings. Perhaps speculating on it leads to madness. But then there is Freemasonry. Freemasonry will not let me discuss religion or politics, but it will let me ask Why?

To become a Master Mason you must learn about balance, about emotion, about intellect and about ego. Only then can you face up to the question Why? And what answer does Freemasonry provide?

Bro. Walter Wilmshurst said:

In the last resource no one can communicate the deeper things in Masonry to another. Every man must discover and learn them for himself, although a friend or brother may be able to conduct him a certain distance on the path of understanding. We know that even the elementary and superficial secrets of the Order must not be communicated to unqualified persons, and the reason for this injunction is not so much because those secrets have any special value, but because that silence is intended to be typical of that which applies to the greater, deeper secrets, some of which, for appropriate reasons, must not be communicated, and some of which indeed are not communicable at all, because they transcend the power of communication.

How far the Masonic Craft on earth reflects, and is over-shadowed and inspired by the hierarchies of that Grand Lodge Above to which the text of our teaching so expressly alludes, must remain a matter of private belief or personal consciousness for each of us, according to our perception or experience. But with some of us at least the conviction is profound that, moving behind the terrestrial organization of the Craft, are directive Powers calling it to higher purposes than it has not yet fulfilled, and shaping it into fuller accordance with the plans of the Master Architect of all. And this faith provides the greatest of all our motives for laying our hand to the work that has been begun today.

This is the core Masonic teaching about matters of private belief which allows the Scientist Mason first to ask the question Why? And then to answer Freemasonry. This answer is a metaphor for the way the Craft allows us to approach the centre of our being and to contemplate possible reasons for our existence. Let me quote Bro. Wilmshurst again:

Here we are in a Lodge, close-tiled against intrusion from without. We are appropriately ranged at the circumference. Each one's back is significantly turned upon the outside world; he is precluded even from looking out into it; his face and attention are averted from everything external and directed towards a common centre where there is emptiness and nothing, save the sacred symbol which signifies Everything.

Could there be any more eloquent device to suggest to us the fact that our very posture in the Lodge implies that we are meant to be engaged collectively in the task of turning our minds inwards upon our own common Centre and trying to bridge the distance lying between us at the circumference and it?

When I take part in a lodge my single idea is the contemplation of the Centre, my only aim to experience that which is symbolised by the empty emblem at the centre of the building and what it can awaken in the Temple of my own mind. I want to feel the light of my personal Centre shine within me as I turn from that which is without to that which is within. I want it to flood and irradiate my whole being, so that I cease to exist on the circumference of consciousness and instead become one with my Centre. I want to understand if I have a purpose.

Masonry offers me a route into the darkness which hides at the centre of my own self-awareness, it gives me the courage to approach it and empowers me to permit entanglement with the eternal wisdom of the void so that I become strong enough to ask why am I?

And it also gives me the inner harmony to face the possibility of an awesome dark emptiness in the answer.

Essay 4 - The Nature of Masonic Truth

The ritual answer to the question "What are the three grand principles on which Freemasonry is founded?" is "Brotherly love, Relief, and Truth." We all think we know what Brotherly love is. It is the warm feeling of fellowship and goodwill we get when we take part in the rituals of our own lodge, the comradeship we share when we dine together after the meeting. We also understand the simple meaning of Relief, the giving of alms and support of those in need. But do we understand Truth? And could we explain to a newly made brother the real nature of Masonic Truth?

As Freemasons we understand that we are taking part in a search for Truth but is Masonic Truth different from common or garden truth?

And will understanding any difference tell us something about Freemasonry?

Masonic Truth must be more than the straightforward conformity with fact or reality that constitutes scientific truth, or even the legal definition of the true or actual state of a matter. So what might it be?

I believe that Masonic Truth must be something which is discovered through practicing the rituals of the Craft and that those rituals allow a freedom of interpretation which makes room for each individual to have a different concept of Masonic Truth.

This view emphasizes the need to learn the ritual thoroughly so that neither you, nor the other lodge members, are worrying about getting the all right words in the right order. The ritual should be learned so thoroughly that that you can deliver it like an artist singing a well-rehearsed song. The words should be automatic, but the feeling and intonation will make a delivery sublime. When you stop worrying about the words the emotions and feelings that the ritual is meant to evoke can work its magic on both you and the rest of your lodge. In this way it helps each brother perceive the deeper mysteries it is meant to illuminate.

Every individual brother may well be like one of that mythical group of blind men each feeling different parts of an elephant and describing it variously as a tree-truck, a snake or a hard pointed spike, depending on whether they were feeling the leg, the truck or the tusks. What they feel and what that feeling causes the ritual words to invoke in their mind will be different each time for each brother. And this, of course, means that there might be no absolute Masonic Truth. But the Masonic quest for Truth is a state of mind that can accommodate a great deal of uncertainty.

Life is always uncertain and once we realize that we live in a state of uncertainty we ought to be ready to admit it both to ourselves and to others. As physicist Richard Feynman said. 'It is of great value to realize that we do not know the answers to difficult questions. This attitude of mind – this attitude of uncertainty- is vital to the scientist and it is this attitude of mind which the student of science must acquire'. This open and questioning attitude to truth is what a Freemason is trying to acquire. Once a scientist develops this attitude to scientific truth they can never again retreat into certainty. The same is probably true for a Freemason.

This is why Masonic truth is different from religious truth. Religion demands a certainty of belief that directly conflicts with the change and growth inherent in the Masonic experience of Truth. Masonic Truth flows from our perception of the ritual. In that way Masonic Truth is much nearer the vision of truth sought by quantum physics. My key philosophy of science is that accepted knowledge is only the best guess I can make at this time. A new fact can change my view. As a scientist I live in a state of perpetual uncertainty. Impartial observations decide the validity of a scientific assertion, but there are no absolute truths, I can only fail to disprove an hypothesis, never show it to be absolutely true.

Freemasonry works in a similar way and although I may experience an insight about my self, through contemplation or the working of a ritual. That insight is something which only exists within me and is almost impossible to convey accurately to somebody else. Religion deals with questions such as 'would it be right to do this thing?', which are outside the competence of science but then it makes pronouncements that cannot be questioned. However such questions are not beyond the scope of Freemasonry, which admits that it is a singular type of morality. Freemasonry exposes you to the emotions, arguments and personal interactions with key events in human experience, but it does not proscribe how you must understand or use the insight you gain from this process.

To follow an idea, it must first engage your heart. You must be inspired. To reason it through, to understand and apply it you must question, analyze and doubt. Where do you seek for a source of strength and courage to persevere in this daunting search for Truth? Traditionally religion provided that inspiration, while science's role was to provide the working tools to understand and share insights. But in today's society this accommodation is seriously weakened.

When religion demands a certainty of belief it directly conflicts with the inherent uncertainty, which is an essential part of science and so it does not reveal truth. When religion ventures into questions of 'how does this work?' then its certainty becomes its weakness. Then the doubting uncertainty of science exposes its flaws and calls into it into question. Freemasonry moderates these two approaches. It uses the techniques of ritual and symbolism to provide a science of the human spirit to guide the seeker towards insights which make sense and it sets its teachings within an ethical framework which does not rely on superstition to enforce it.

The Masonic teacher, Bro Walter Wilmshurst writing in 1904, said.

To understand how Science and Religion express opposite sides of the same fact, the one its near or visible side, the other its remote or invisible side, is our problem. How to find this harmony, how to reconcile the two, is the question to be answered. We have to seek out that ultimate truth which both will avow with absolute sincerity. But, if the two are to be reconciled, the basis of reconciliation must be this deepest, widest, and most certain of all facts – that the Power which the Universe manifests to us is utterly inscrutable . . . as we scan the scientific horizon and watch the accumulating portents of the times, as we piece together fragments of new knowledge that are coming out of the laboratories, and study the deductions that speculative thought is drawing from that new knowledge, it is possible to venture upon some provisional forecast. And what will be the effect of the new disclosure upon religious thought and belief? Will it tend, as the increase of scientific knowledge has hitherto done, to the further rout and destruction of ideals of faith? Or will it tend to restore and strengthen them?

Wilmshurst wrote the above just four years after Max Planck speculated that all energy might be split into discrete packets, and a full year before Albert Einstein discovered the mathematics that explained how that could be and kick-started the quantum revolution in physics.

Bro. Walter continued:

The theories of Science, like the dogmas of Theology, are mere working hypotheses; conclusions drawn from certain premises, and capable of adjustment to the demands of increased knowledge as knowledge itself increases. Gravitation cannot be proved any more than the Incarnation; evolution is an inference as much as the doctrine of the Trinity; the ether a postulate as necessary a basis for scientific thought as the existence of a Deity is a basis essential to the practice of religious thought. In each case certain assumptions are necessary, and these assumptions may differ at different times, but in any case Science is as dogmatic as Theology, and Theology as theoretical as Science; and no finality is practicable for either. . . . Hence, there must always be a place for Religion, which under all its forms is distinguished from everything else in that its subject matter is something that passes the sphere of ordinary experience. Science, on the other hand, is simply the higher development of common knowledge. But if both Religion and Science have bases in the reality of things, then between them there must be a fundamental harmony. There cannot be two orders of Truth in absolute and everlasting opposition.

For me Masonic Truth is a truth which stirs my heart, while still making sense in my head. It is a truth I want to believe in, as well as one I can reason my way to accepting.

The lodge trains you in experiencing and thinking about truth, it also provides a forum to share truth, it offers opportunities to demonstrate truth and chances to work together to provide group experiences of truth. In this way regular participation in working Masonic ritual can help you internalize truth, so that you can make a daily advancement in Masonic knowledge.

It is, however, for you to decide what constitutes your Masonic Truth. Perhaps it is a subject you may care make the focus your regular meditation so you make your own progress up the spiral stairway of nature and science.

Essay 5 - The Quest for Masonic Illumination

After the first informal meeting of the Lodge of Living Stones, under the new mastership of Bro. Tony Baker, a few of the brethren ended up in the lounge at Castle Grove. We found ourselves discussing the subject of illumination, when used in a Masonic context.

"What do you think Masonic illumination means within the traditions of the Lodge of Living Stones," Tony asked me.

"I'm not really sure," I replied, "But wouldn't it make a good subject for an essay?"

So that is why I decided to investigate the teachings of Bro. Walter Leslie Wilmshurst. the founding master of our research lodge, on this matter and then add my own comments to the question.

Bro. Wilmshurst has written about the topic of light and he linked it to spiritual power. He said.

Our system teaches that the currents of spiritual power and light is always favourable to Masonry when coming from either East or West... It is traditional, that the four specially favourable times are at midwinter, midsummer, and at the vernal and autumnal equinoxes, but that of these four the most favourable of all is midwinter. It is on this account that the four official meetings of the Lodge have been fixed for those four seasons, and Installation ceremonies are timed for midwinter. For light is born at the moment of maximum darkness. At midwinter the currents of cosmic energy renew their constructive work in the sap of vegetation and in human vital forces, and the solar light begins to increase.

When I first visited the Lodge of Living Stones, and long before I ever read the words I have quoted above, I was impressed that the lodge met at the four turning points of the solar year. It met near the winter solstice, when light is severely restricted, at the two equinoxes when light and dark are in perfect balance, and at the summer solstice which light seems never quite to disappear from Northern sky. The lodge symbolically travels from the darkness of midwinter, through the first balance point of day and night to the high point of summer brightness, before slowly relaxing back through the harmony of the autumnal equinox back into winter darkness as it prepares to renew itself at Installation. Its meeting times follow an ancient inspirational cycle which reflects by the progress of time and the balance of day and night, the black and white squares of our temple pavement.

In his inaugural address to the Lodge of Living Stones, on 16th December 1927, Bro. Wilmshurst described Freemasonry as a quest to find the eternal light of the soul, which I can only interpret as a search for Masonic illumination. These are his actual words.

Every true Masonic candidate contemplating entry into the mysteries of our Craft should, in truth, be an idealist engaged in the never-ending quest for perfection and union with the Divine. He must lull the promptings of the exterior life and open the door of the soul; he must resign himself to the mysteries of the Presence in which we all live and move, and, as a true disciple and enlightened pupil of our ancient mysteries, listen to its mystic promptings and respond to it in the language of the soul, which is made to rise to Truth upon the stepping stones of error and imperfection, and to find the eternal light when its own light has failed. The work of the spiritual Craftsman is a practical and scientific necessity. In his upward expression the aim of the true mystic is essentially union with God, a union which is not merely psychological, but ontological. The Masonic disciple will, in his deep meditation, exclaim, "from the unreal lead me to the real, from darkness lead me to light, from the mortal bring me to immortality." It is manifest how large is the path of light, and how in everything which is felt or known God himself is latent, though the veil is still present yet the light in which we live shines through the veil. By it our souls are illuminated and guided into all truth and wisdom. With this longing for the revelation of supernatural light and union with the divine, the true initiate can become a master-soul, and when that light within him is dimmed, he will exclaim "O re-kindle in me, Light of the World!"

He goes on to link the quest for light to a search for Divine Wisdom saying.

Brethren, do not turn your feet away from the Divine Wisdom which presents us with the most soul-satisfying harmonies and is the *Vade-mecum* concerning those unutterable mysteries which are a lamp to the feet and a light on the path. Masonry is the most appealing working philosophy; it is the teaching of a diviner spirit than man's. And if it has upon it the mark of the prentice-hand, yet, for those who will see with open eyes, it has also the imprint of the finger of God.

Bro. Wilmshurst likens the quest for Truth, to a search for what he calls Divine Wisdom, and symbolizes it as a lamp to light the way through a path of darkness. This darkness shrouds the mystery of existence. Why do we live and what is the purpose of intelligent life? Bro. Wilmshurst challenges us to face up to the mystery of our existence, both physical and intellectual. We exhorts us to seek for a foothold of stability and peace and to help throw light upon our problems and guide us to what he calls "the secret keys to the mystery of life".

Bro. Wilmshurst teaches that the first inclination a Craftsman has of the nature of his search for this glimmer of light in the East is something the second degree is designed to inculcate. He said that the Craft was specially designed to lead us to study "the hidden mysteries of nature and science," and so to develop "knowledge of yourself" as the most important of all human studies.

He warns that a high standards of compliance with the Moral Law are an indispensable preliminary requisite for any Brother who ventures to pursue the hidden mysteries of nature and the spiritual science of his own deeper being. Bro. Wilmshurst says that only when you have been disciplined to a high state of morality and virtue, developed physical and mental self-control, and gained detachment from worldly possessions and ideals, by the practice of self-giving instead of self-getting, should you be permitted to extend your researches into the deeply hidden things. He says that:

A secret Order, with solemn dedicatory prayers, with obligations of secrecy, and references to the attainment of a higher than earthly wisdom, and expressing itself in solemnities is not needed to teach morality; it is desirable for organized effort to promote a sacred, secret science dealing with the mysteries of being and the quest of Reality or what we call "the Centre."

Here for the first time we see a clue as to the source of Masonic illumination. But he left us a further reminder in the Noon Day prayer which all members of the lodge are encouraged pause and silently recite at the hour of high twelve. Here the subject of Masonic illumination takes centre stage. Bro. Wilmshurst's Noon Day Prayer says.

Here, in the presence of the Great Architect and in fellowship with my Brother Masons, I offer myself as a living stone of a building raised to the service of God and the Craft.

May the power of the Highest overshadow and descend upon us! May Light illumine and Love unite us, that we may know ourselves one in God, and that from our unity there may go forth to all beings Light, Love, Peace !

But what is the light that we can only bring forth when we act in unity with our brethren to act as a living stone of the temple raised to the service of God and the Craft? This is the source of the

Masonic illumination which the Lodge of Living Stones exists to make visible in the darkness.

Bro. Wilmshurst explained more about this glimmer of light which flickers at our centre when he wrote.

Man has an inside personality; a large psychological field usually called the Soul, which animates and actuates the outside self, but is far larger, more subtle and complex than the latter. It bears exactly the same relation to the outside self as the interior of the Lodge does to its exterior; and it is to the mysteries of this interior man - the human soul - which survives when its body dies, that the science of the Craft is entirely directed. The Lodge is formed as it is with the direct purpose of serving as a visible model of that sphere of psychical faculties and tendencies which we call the Soul, and to show how by the discipline of the Craft this inner man of each of us may be developed from a state of chaos to one of order and beauty, be wrought from the rough ashlar to the perfect cube, and be transformed from its natural darkness into supernatural light. And just as the outer body of man has to be opened for physiological investigation, so the Lodge also is " opened " that we may behold the constitution of our inner self and understand its mechanism and purpose.

The Spirit indwells the Soul, just as the Soul suffuses the Body; but only in the Soul which is rectified, purified and worked from the rough ashlar to the perfect cube condition can it, as the "Centre," be brought to life and consciousness in the mind. To achieve this is the work of the Craft Mason, and its achievement means Mastership. The Master of a Lodge, as the apex of all within it, is emblematically the point at which the divine Spirit is in contact with the Soul, and from which the Light-vibrations from above stream into the Lodge of the Soul, permeating and illumining all the latter's faculties and properties, and penetrating even to the external personality.

When we join together with our brethren to form a perfect lodge we create an opportunity for the glimmer of light in the East, represented by the Master of the lodge, to shine into the corporate soul of the lodge and illuminate us all with the suprenal light of the Centre.

When we form a lodge we come together to conduct our Candidates on the path of Light so that in the darkness of the circumferance we may be illuminated by the glory of the light from the Centre. The Master and Wardens make up a trinity of lesser lights illuminating the lodge by reflecting the light from the Centre into the lodge so that our souls may unite, in emulation of the Great Architect, to build a temple of immortality which is wreathed with Light as if by a garment.

I would sum up Bro. Wilmshurst's teaching on Masonic illumination by quoting him. "Without the Light and Wisdom of the Spirit, the soul of man is darkness and his body of flesh a thing of nought; and, without soul and body as its instruments, the Spirit abides in itself. But the Great Architect has joined these three together and appointed the Spirit as a wise master-builder to rule over soul and body, that from these imperfect corruptible materials may be erected an immortal House of Light wherein The Most High may tabernacle with man."

This teaching is summed up in the ritual words Bro. Wilmshurst wrote for the Immediate Past Master of the Lodge to read out and explain his role. The IPM sits in silence in the East of the Lodge to assist in the opening and closing and to give charges and counsel to the brethren when needed. But he also sums up how the progressive nature of the Craft is illuminated as the Mason moves progressively through the offices.

"I sit in the perpetual Light of the East," the IPM says, "And gaze back into the West, whence, long ago I was moved in my heart to set forth and seek for that which was lost to me. And now, by God's help and my own industry, I have found it! For me all hoodwinks have been lifted, all veils removed, and to-day the sight of my soul is keen. With enlarged vision I behold the world as a vast Lodge wherein Divine Mysteries are celebrated perpetually, whereof those of our Craft are an image. I perceive all life as a procession entering at the West and journeying to the East, ascending from the dust of the earth to the heights of heaven and I know the Mysteries of Our Brotherhood to be a means of grace divinely appointed to help men on their way."

"Brethren," the IPM finishes. "This is the conclusion of the Mysteries of the Craft, and after this manner shall they be fulfilled in every one who turns from darkness to light. Ponder them in silence, for in silence are the Mysteries fulfilled and illuminated."

The Master knocks his gavel, the lights are lowered and the lodge sits in silence to ponder the lost mysteries of the Craft which have just be so poetically expounded.

Personally I use the opening dark silence to still my body and mind. In this second dark silence I allow myself to focus on the purpose of the Cosmic Plan which underpins the reality I study as a scientist and I muse on how I might better understand and apply it. Our late organist Bro. George Fildes once told me that sometimes during the second dark silence of the fulfilled lodge he saw the light of the centre filling the whole of the temple and he felt an innate awe of the Infinite.

The writings of Bro. Wilmshurst have taught me that the fullness of the human mind is like a lodge, which I can learn to open and enter. But I have also been cautioned that within that lodge there is darkness as well as light. The closing prayer warns of the joys and perils to be encountered in my personal lodge as I struggle to move from darkness to light.

Be unto us the Lesser Warden, and in the meridian sunlight of our understanding speak to us in sacraments that shall declare the splendours of Thy unmanifested light;

Be Thou also unto us the Greater Warden, and in the awful hour of disappearing light, when vision fails and thought has no more strength, be with us still, revealing to us, as we may bear them, the hidden mysteries of Thy shadow;

And so through light and darkness, raise us, Great Master, till we are made one with Thee, in the unspeakable glory of Thy presence in the East.

These few ritual words sum up the paradox of the secret knowledge of Masonic illumination that lies within each Brother. When sacraments speak to me I stand amid the splendours of unmanifested light but when my thoughts lose strength I must face the terrors of the night. Such are the perils that beset me when I turn from that which is without, to join with my lodge brethren to magnify and focus the glory of light that can blossom from the faint spark that is within us all.

Essay 6 - The Corporate Identity of the Perfect Lodge

During the consecration of the Lodge of Living Stones, its founding master Bro. Walter Wilmshurst said:

The direction of inquiry .. towards matters to which the Craft was specially designed to lead us... are... "the hidden mysteries of nature and science," ... involving that "knowledge of yourself" which... is ... the most important of all human studies. ...These matters go far beyond the mere "system of morality" which the Order also... provides... In our system, it is not until the neophyte Mason has been disciplined to a high state of morality and virtue, has been trained in physical and mental self-control, been educated in detachment from ordinary worldly possessions and ideals, and habituated to the practice of self-giving instead of self-getting, that, as we say, he is " permitted to extend his researches" into more deeply hidden things. And it is at this point that the "system of morality" opens out... into a system of Initiation-science.

He went on to say "The first lesson imparted to Candidates for Initiation in all ages was Know Thyself, since truly to know oneself involves a knowledge of all else even of The Great Architect, in whom everything lives, moves, and has its being."

Here are two major clues to the secret knowledge which has to be hunted out before you can emerge from the darkness, which you impose on yourself, and become aware of the faint glimmer of light which beckons to you towards the East.

In preparing a Candidate for this revelation of the "more deeply hidden things" of our Craft, the lodge has first to help him through a series of trials and tests of merit. The disciplines of morality, virtue, self-control, and self-giving are not easy to acquire and often, even though we feel we have mastered them, when we are put to the test by a brother's "unreasonable" behaviour we find that we can not live up to our professed intentions. At these times we discover things inside us of which we are unaware. Much as we like to believe we are in control of ourselves we often find we are not. What we say and how we behave are not in harmony, and our mind is not in balance.

We are told, from Bro Wilmshurst's writings in The Book of the Perfect Lodge, that the fullness of the human mind is like a lodge, which we can learn to open and enter. But we are also warned that within that lodge there is darkness as well as light. This is the paradox of the secret knowledge we seek. When sacraments speak to us we stand amid the splendours of unmanifested light but when thought has no more strength we face the terrors of the night. Such are the perils that beset us when we turn from that which is without to that which is within.

Words and thought are the natural tools we hope to use when we set out in search of our inner Truth. And they will carry us a long way along our journey from West to East, before they finally fail us. Much of our Craft is founded on words. Our ritual is built on words and we jealously guard each and every particular one as it is reverently spoken aloud above the echoing silence of the temple pavement. No matter which brother speaks his lodge brethren each echo his words in the silent spaces of their own souls, each copying his example within the personal lodge of their mind. We vehemently shun the substituted secrets of synonyms and disdain the false vision of extended verbal explanation. For only when our inner and outer lodges unite as a single voice do we feel at one with our brethren. And this only happens when they too seek internal tranquility so that the harmony of the inner and outer lodges is not disturbed. Yet before we engage in silent and intimate union with the ritual words, we prepare ourselves by stilling our thoughts. We lower the lights and let darkness flood our temple so that the splendour of the light will not distract us from the silence of unspoken sacraments.

The paradox of our search for light is that we must first learn to embrace our dread of darkness to prepare ourselves to work with that love and harmony which should at all times characterize a Perfect Lodge. When we withdraw from the intimate fellowship of shared understanding which open lodge provides, and prepare to return to the normal world, we first sojourn awhile in individual darkness. This allows the new fragment of shared Truth to veil itself in shadow so that its brilliance will not dazzle us into incomprehension. So our experience of light and darkness, of thought and fear, are made one as we prepare to exit the Temple and pass out beneath the portal of holy mysteries.

This is how we build the spiritual capital of the lodge. A lodge meeting is not a ceremonial spectacle, it is a means of leading each individual brother towards the shared knowledge held by the corporate spirit which is the Prefect Lodge. Each successive meeting of a Perfect Lodge will increase the palpable atmosphere which Masonic practice should engender so that it will always feel good to enter the lodge - for members, for candidates and for visitors.

Bro. Walter reminds us that the purpose of a Perfect Lodge is to forge a connecting link between the Lodge of Brethren in this world and the invisible hierarchies, so that a channel might be formed for an unobstructed current of spiritual energy between the Great Architect, in the light of the Eternal East, and the Perfect Lodge, in the Earth's lengthening shadow of the West.

This message is not one which the modern scientific mind has been trained to accept. It is not a testable material message rather it is an esoteric enigma. But he who is not prepared to be open to things he does not know will not find out the unexpected, for the unknown is trackless and unexplored. The nature of Truth is contradictory and whenever we try to capture it in language we are inevitably drawn into paradox, yet all attempts to avoid paradox lead to distortions of Truth. This is why the lodge works in darkness and in light, by individual reflection and by corporate re-iteration. Truth lies in the deep structure of the world and is experienced by thought and by awe, by reason and by intuition. What we experience is more certain than what other people tell us about what they have experienced. But most people do not understand what they experience, so experience is not enough on its own. The Craft offers training in experiencing and thinking about Truth, it offers a forum to share Truth, it offers opportunities to demonstrate Truth and times to work together to provide group experiences of Truth. In this way brethren are helped to internalize Truth so that we may each make a daily advancement in Masonic knowledge.

Bro. Walter reminds us that the strength and worth of a lodge does not depend upon numbers and popular attractions, but upon the quality and intensity of the corporate life of its members, upon their united and consistent co-operation towards a common ideal, and upon their ability to form a "group-mind" or "group-consciousness". We experience this group-mind not when we open the corporate lodge together, but between the dark silences which delineate our inner working. Before we work our ceremony we lower the veil of darkness to encourage us to open the inner lodge of our own consciousness ready to allow to it resonate with the inner lodges of our brethren so that the open corporate lodge becomes a grand lodge of inner lodges. It is this grand lodge of personal inner lodges that is the group mind of the corporate lodge. Then after the work of the ceremony is done, we lower the lights to afford us the privacy of darkness whilst we close our inner lodges before sharing in the closing of the corporate lodge.

But as our corporate lodge does not meet daily, if we are to work each day on the smoothing and squaring of the Living Stone we plan to offer to the fabric of the Temple, then we need to do more that just attend each month. Bro, Walter has left us a way when he invited us to co-operate actively and systematically with the rest of our brethren to form an organic unity of minds, not merely a temporary association of persons. He tells us that we should follow the guidance of Grand Master Hiram Abif and at the hour of high-twelve banish every other thought and visualize our

Perfect Lodge together, in peace, concord, and charity.

To follow his guidance, at high twelve seek out a quiet place. Close your eyes to feel the comradely warmth of the dark silence as you tyle and open your personal inner lodge. Then in the silent temple of your soul let your Eternal Spirit of Wisdom address the brethren of your body, mind and spirit thus:

Here, in the presence of the Great Architect and in fellowship with my Brother Masons, I offer myself as a living stone of a building raised to the service of God and the Craft.

May the power of the Highest overshadow and descend upon us! May Light illumine and Love unite us, that we may know ourselves one in God, and that from our unity there may go forth to all beings Light, Love, Peace !

And you will feel the fellowship of the Perfect Lodge grow within, as you experience Truth.

Essay 7 - The Purposes of the Dark Silence

When the Lodge of Living Stones was consecrated our first Master Bro. Walter Leslie Wilmshurst said.

For the purpose of establishing spiritual contact with, and receiving influxes from the Higher Powers, four specially favourable times are midwinter, midsummer, and the vernal and autumnal equinoxes. Of these the most favourable is midwinter. This is why the four official meetings of the Lodge have been fixed for those four seasons, and why the Consecration and Installation ceremonies are timed for midwinter.

Light is born at the moment of maximum darkness. At midwinter the currents of cosmic energy renew their constructive work in the sap of vegetation and in human vital forces. The solar light begins to increase.

He was aware of the symbolic significance of experiencing darkness in order to appreciate light. To mark this he introduced into our lodge ritual a special feature known as the dark silence. The first silence is held after the opening of the lodge to enable the brethren to prepare themselves to submerge their individual egos into a fully integrated lodge ready to carry out the work required of it. The second silence is carried out just before the lodge is closed to allow the brethren to reflect on what they have just achieved by working together. The ritual instructions say:

THE SILENCE

The WM will invite the Brn to join him in silent meditation. The main lights are turned down and almost off. At the conclusion of the Silence, the WM will give one quiet K; the lights are turned back up.

In *The Lost Key* I wrote about how profound an experience it was for me when I first experienced one as a visitor. This is what I said:

The opening ceremony of the lodge was more complex than anything I had seen before. They performed a ritual of lighting the officers' candles which involved lighting a taper from an eternal flame at the centre of the lodge and carrying the light to its periphery. The Master announced that the lodge was going to work a ritual lecture, known as The Book of the Perfect Lodge, which had been devised by their founding Master Bro. W. L. Wilmshurst to explain the purpose of a lodge and how it should work together to fulfill its purpose. Then, to my surprise, the master announced that we would spend a few minutes in silence whilst we prepared ourselves for the task. I was even more surprised when the lights were lowered, and everyone fell quiet. For two or three minutes we sat in a dark, rich silence. I felt myself getting calmer and more focused. The faint, flickering light of the four candles, one by each of the officers' pedestals and one high in the centre of the lodge, reminded me of the darkness of my Third Degree. As I listened to the deep breathing of the otherwise silent men surrounding me I could hear the rhythm of their respiration moving towards an harmonious concord.

The Master knocked with his gavel, and the light was gently restored. The temple was calm and alert. The Master began by explaining the purpose of the ritual.

'A Lodge is much more than an assembly of persons,' he began. "When duly formed and opened it represents the inner working of each individual Mason who is a part of it. It is purposely designed as to be an object lesson in that most interesting of human studies, the knowledge of yourself. For the true work of the Craft, that of disciplining and perfecting yourself, cannot be undertaken until you know what your self is." (Lomas, 2012)

Since that first dramatic experience I have attended many dark silences and have come to appreciate what they can offer. In this essay I intend to explore how the practice of the dark silence benefits an individual brother.

A mysterious bridge connects the visible and the invisible, joins that which is without to that which is within. That bridge is your material body, which enables you to live, and sustains your mind and spirit. Control of your body is one path to help access the inner knowledge of your soul. As a baby you learned a great deal about your mother's emotions by imitating her posture and facial movements, only later discovering what feelings were associated with these bodily expressions. The ritual of the lodge of Living Stones aids the acquisition of self-knowledge by encouraging us to pay careful attention to bodily postures and gestures, for control over your body is the first step in gaining control over your thinking function. Uncontrolled agitation of the body inevitably produces uncontrollable agitation of the mind, and that precludes serious study of your inner world. The ritual of the dark silence enforces stillness and calm on both lodge members and visitors alike.

Once a high degree of inner calmness and quietude has been established and the continually bustling activity of the mind stilled, the centre can become visible in the darkness. This is called bringing about clarity of vision or making darkness visible. Those who have no personal experience of this higher level of awareness cannot imagine it, and the language of those who try to explain it often means nothing, it is almost impossible to put into words and any attempt may seem to be a sign of incipient madness.

Within new age circles there is much talk about the attainment of `higher states of consciousness'. Unfortunately this aspiration does not always grow out of deep respect for the great wisdom traditions, the world religions or Masonic teachings. Often it is based on an inability to distinguish between the spiritual and the occult. Sadly such individuals are seeking new thrills, to master magic and miracles, or enliven their existential boredom. This is never the intention, or result, of practicing a dark silence within the open lodge. My advice is not to chase occult experiences and not to pay too undue attention to them when they seem to occur – as they most inevitably will when any intensive inner work is undertaken. I have experienced these spectacular visions and find they are easily explained in terms the mechanisms of physics acting on the brain.

Such events are superficial indications of a change in mental state, rather than an objective to strive for. The calm awareness of your inner nature and expansion of your awareness of the universe is but one of the paths to Truth. Sharing in the spirit of a living lodge during a dark silence is another.

In my opinion, Living Stones is not seeking to elucidate showy responses, testaments of strange experiences, or occult knowledge. Its purpose is to help you reach into yourself, deep into the source of your self-awareness, and to access the hidden knowledge which is to be found there. So how do you learn to approach your own inner depths? Let me share with you how I conduct my dark silences.

I begin by taking three deep breaths. I breath in deeply, but comfortably through my nose, counting to ten as I do so. I hold the breath in for a further slow count of ten and then breath out through my mouth to yet another count of ten. I repeat this three times to establish a rhythm of deep slow breathing. Once I have achieved this, I systematically relax my body. I direct my attention, first to my feet, feeling them heavy again the floor, then move upwards to feel my legs, my thighs, my torso up to my arms. I feel for tightness and try to release it into slackness. Finally I reach my head. I consciously relax my neck muscles, allow the tension to slip away from my jaw and my eyes. Then, with my body calm and still, I focus on my mind. I look at the faint shadow of the black and white pavement and fix it, along my bodily state, in my memory. I do this so that I can visit that memory when I join in the noonday prayer so that I can feel the spirit of the lodge enfolding me.

Now I focus on stilling my mind. I think only of the dark pavement and the quietness of the eternal flame flickering faintly above its centre. As I have usually come to lodge after a full day at the university my mind will be bubbling with memories, ideas and random connections. Each time my mind starts to chase one of these mental flickerings I pull it back to contemplate the darkness of the centre. Slowly I find my mind becoming still.

Sometimes I achieve inner stillness before the master knocks for the lights to be raised, sometimes I don't, but I am always much calmer and more focused by the end of the silence. Now I am prepared to listen actively to the forthcoming paper or take a full part in the ceremony, depending on what work the lodge has set itself that evening.

In the closing dark silence I follow the same procedure of stilling and calming my body. When I am consciously relaxed, I again focus on the flickering light of the eternal flame at the centre and whilst allowing my mind to dwell on the work we have just done. I dissemble what I have heard or experienced, and review it as it drifts gently across my mind. The points which have made most impression on me float to the surface and by reviewing them I commit them to my store of memories for future contemplation. The quiet knock of the master always takes me by surprise as I find I have become deeply involved in assimilating the lessons of our meeting. The dark silence is always followed immediately by the closing prayer, which grabs my attention as the lights of the lodge are raised. This lodge prayer was written by Bro. Wilmshurst for the use of any Mason. It goes.

Oh Sovereign and Most Worshipful of all Masters, who, in Thy infinite love and wisdom, hast devised our Order as a means to draw Thy children nearer Thee, and hast so ordained its Officers that they are emblems of Thy seven-fold power, Be Thou unto us an Outer Guard, and defend us from the perils that beset us when we turn from that which is without to that which is within ;

Be Thou unto us an Inner Guard, and preserve our souls that desire to pass within the portal of Thy holy mysteries ;

Be unto us the Younger Deacon, and teach our wayward feet the true and certain steps upon the path that leads to Thee :

Be Thou also the Elder Deacon, and guide us up the steep and winding stairway to Thy throne ;

Be unto us the Lesser Warden, and in the meridian sunlight of our understanding speak to us in sacraments that shall declare the splendours of Thy unmanifested light;

Be Thou also unto us the Greater Warden, and in the awful hour of disappearing light, when vision fails and thought has no more strength, be with us still, revealing to us, as we may bear them, the hidden mysteries of Thy shadow;

And so through light and darkness, raise us, Great Master, till we are made one with Thee, in the unspeakable glory of Thy presence in the East.

So mote it be.

The dark silences punctuate the start and ending of a state of corporate identity within the lodge. During the first dark silence we cast aside the cares and worries of our daily lives and concentrate on working together as a lodge to the best of our ability. During the second dark silence we separate our souls from the corporate soul of the lodge and take with us a sense of spiritual refreshment into the outer world to sustain us until we can meet again as a lodge of Living Stones.

Essay 8 - The Importance of a Questioning Attitude

When you first knocked on the door of the lodge and asked to be admitted you were asked a question. "Who comes there?"

That is the first of many and varied ritual questions which you meet as you progress through the system of The Craft. You were not expected to answer that first question yourself. The Tyler spoke on your behalf, but once inside the lodge you were encouraged to answer personally.

The first question "Are you free by birth and of the full age of 21?", should have been easy to answer in the affirmative as our modern society does not sanction the keeping of slaves and Freemasonry affirms that all its members are equal. But then the probing went deeper. You were asked. "In all times of danger and difficulties, in whom do you put your trust?" You were prompted to answer "In God." In this way you were questioned to see if you believed that some form of organizing principle govened the universe. And it is perfectly acceptable, for the physicists among us, to trust in a God who has a gambling problem in sub-atomic dealings, provided we can accept that on a cosmic scale there is purpose to be studied. As Newton said when describing the role of Great Architect in *Principia Mathematica*.

The most beautiful system of the sun, planets, and comets, could only proceed from the counsel and dominion of an intelligent and powerful being. And if the fixed stars are the centres of like systems, these, being formed by the like wise counsel, must be all subjects to the dominion of one; especially since the light of the fixed stars is of the same nature with the light of the sun, and from every system light passes into all the other systems; and lest the systems of fixed stars should, by their gravity, fall on each other, he hath placed those systems at immense distances from one another.

This being governs all things, not as the soul of the world, but as Lord over all; and on account of his dominion he is wont to be called the Lord God or Universal Ruler, for God is a relative word, and has a respect to servants; and Deity is the dominion of God not over his own body, as those imagine who fancy God to be the soul of the world, but over servants. The Supreme Being is eternal, infinite, absolutely perfect, omnipotent and omniscient. ...

We know him only by his most wise and excellent contrivances of things and final causes.

Newton had been inspired as young man by the questioning attitude of John Wallis, a Freemason who helped found the Royal Society, along with Bro. Sir Robert Moray. But Bro Wallis also developed the advanced method of using symbols to pose and answer questions that we now call algebra. Since the time of Plato, over two thousand years ago, Masons and builders have believed that there is a source of pure symbols existing in a spiritual realm of perfection. Plato taught that with careful training an individual could be shown how to communicate with this realm and discover the true nature of these symbols. He developed this thought into a theory of ideas and it is a way of thinking which is deeply embedded in the Masonic system of self-improvement. Freemasonry practices a basic method of teaching which poses questions, both spoken and implied, that are intended to help Masons to first know themselves and then gain access to the realm of perfect forms.

As an undergraduate at Cambridge University, Newton kept a diary. It reveals that Bro. John Wallis, through his book *Algebra*, shared this Masonic way of thinking, with the young Isaac Newton, by questioning. The book inspired Newton to raise the sort of queries that we Freemasons need to ask ourselves - if we are to progress up the winding stairway of Masonic knowledge.

Let me take, for example, one of the liberal arts we are encouraged to study in our second degree and ask questions about astronomy. Let us reflect on the movements of the Sun and the Moon which Newton was inspired to question. As Masons we are told these heavenly bodies form part of the lesser lights of Freemasonry. They are symbolized by lights burning in the South, the West, and the East, figuratively to represent the Sun, the Moon, and the Master of the Lodge; the Sun to rule the day, the Moon to govern the night and the Master to rule and direct his Lodge.

When we think about the movement of the Moon, our natural inclination is to ask "What keeps it moving across the sky?" But this question is born of the limited nature of the life we lead on the surface of the Earth. We know that a rolling stone will eventually stop rolling and come to rest. By observing this we develop a natural, but mistaken, acceptance that inanimate matter left to itself will always come to rest. So what keeps the Moon moving through the night sky? Kepler suggested it was pushed along by angels, but Newton asked a different question. He realised that friction caused objects to slow down and come to rest. He also suggested that in the perfect realms of heaven there is no friction, and so the Moon continues to move, just as the International Space Station does, without the need for angels to push it along its orbit.

But there is more to the matter of movement. Newton also noticed that if he allowed a bucket of water to twist on the end of a rope the water rose up the sides of the bucket. He extended this idea to notice what happens when a boy swings a conker on the end of a string. It flies outward and traces out a circle. The led him to ask "What makes the water rise up the sides of the rotating bucket?" and "What makes the conker pull away from the boy's hand as he spins it round?" His answer was that whenever an object moves in a circle its velocity changes and any change in velocity, known as an acceleration, produces a force.

Think about pouring a cup of tea in your dining room. It is a fairly simple operation as your dining room is not normally moving. Now think about pouring a cup of tea in a aircraft flying in straight and level flight at a few hundred miles per hour. The task of pouring the tea is just as simple. But now consider what happens if you are in the restaurant car of a train and whilst you are pouring your tea the train brakes hard. You will find the task of hitting the cup with the stream of hot liquid far more difficult. From this we realize that it is changes of velocity which produce forces of movement.

If we return to the question of the movement of the Moon the cause of its movement is a puzzle. If we look in its direction of travel there is nothing to make it move, hence Kepler's suggestion it is being pushed by invisible angels. But once we perceive that the Moon is moving in a circle and remember the direction taken up by the string when the boy swings the conker round his head, then we realize that the force which holds the Moon in place is always directed towards the Earth.

If we extend this idea to ask "What makes the Earth rotate about the Sun on its own axis?" As long as we think something is needed to keep the Earth in motion we look in the direction of the Earth's travel to find the cause, and find a different stellar direction for each season. But if we rotate our view through an angle of ninety degrees (or the fourth part of circle) to the direction of movement we see that the line of gravitational force always points towards the glory of the Sun at the centre.

By changing our question from "What causes the velocity of the Earth? to "What causes the acceleration of the Earth?" we move our focus from the apparently random movements of the sky to see the importance of the Truth at the centre.

So it is with our Masonic progress. Whilst we move around the offices of the lodge we keep our attention fixed only on the direction of preferment. As an Entered Apprentice we look to becoming a Fellow Craft. As Inner Guard we look towards becoming Junior Deacon, as Junior Warden we look to becoming Senior Warden, as Senior Warden we look towards becoming Master. This can become a habit, even when the purposes of progression through the offices had been completed. It can distract us from the real purpose of Freemasonry. By focusing on continual movement through higher and higher offices, we forget that we are only moving around the perimeter of the lodge.

The Truth lies at the centre. Just as the Sun, at the centre of the Solar System, tugs at the Earth as it moves through the cold of empty space, holding it in such a position that it can sustain human life. In like manner the Centre tugs at our souls as we move around the perimeter of the lodge, following the empty rewards of higher office, until we realize that the light of Truth can only to be found by allowing the influence of the Centre to bring our whole being into balance and harmony.

So ask not what Freemasonry can do for you? Instead ask what you can do to help your brethren recognize the true purpose of our Craft, and bring intellect and love into perfect balance by turning towards the Centre.

Essay 9 - Understanding and Practicing Brotherly Love

Freemasonry is based on three grand principles. Brotherly Love, Relief and Truth.

Relief is the easiest of these principles to put into practice. Anonymous giving to charity, practiced by stealth, is a personally rewarding activity which avoids mutually embarrassing encounters with the subjects of your aid. It helps the individual practicing it to feel that they are giving back something to the community which has rewarded them, without any suggestion that their act is motivated by anything other than a selfless wish to help. On a less virtuously sound plane it also can also induce a feeling of moral superiority when listening, without comment or admission of personal action, to brethren talking about what they and their lodge have done for "Charity".

Charity, in modern publicity-hungry Freemasonry, has become a publicly degrading subversion of the principle of Masonic Relief. It taints those who give, as it has the clear intent of demanding to be applauded for something which should be seen as a simple responsibility. Its success is too often measured by the extent of the press coverage achieved. This tarnishes the giver by revealing base motives for what should be an act of secret kindness and it sullies the recipient by forcing a public confession of need and false fealty by acknowledging that the giver has purchased a measure of contrived good-will.

Masonic relief is supposed to be silent and unassuming, requiring no reward but that of knowing that the secret donor has done right and that help has been given. It requires no thanks and if done well should make it impossible to know who to thank. Charity has tended to become an abuse of power and a means of trying to buy undeserved goodwill. Relief should not demand goodwill on the part of the recipient, it is enough that the recipients are in need. Thanks should not be expected and every attempt should be made to ensure that the route by which the Relief is applied remains a secret from the recipient.

Truth is more difficult to practice, as pursing it can lead to the suggestion that "You would rather be right than be liked." This challenge is fair in that to a dedicated Truth seeker it is more important to convey that truth as you understand it, than to follow the views of the crowd. Baying in tune with the mob is comforting but Truth is not democratic. It is not decided by majority opinion but by congruency with facts. Truth can be extremely uncomfortable to hear and the classic response, exemplified in the Masonic tales of King Cyrus, in the back story to the The Royal Arch, is to kill the messengers. It you seek Truth expect to be attacked. If you cannot bear to be criticized then do not study Truth and if you do not want to be vilified avoid speaking Truth to those who do not want to hear. it

This brings me to the question of Brotherly Love. Why should Love matter? Well let me begin by reflecting on the scope of the love which Freemasonry demands of its Craftsman.

Is it limited to our lodge brethren?

Is it limited to our Masonic brethren (both male and female)?

Is it limited to only those human brethren (male and female) who share more than 98% of our genetic makeup?

Or should it extend to every molecule which decides to link valance bonds and form the wonderful spiral chains of DNA which are the characteristic badge of life and the repository of sacred knowledge?

As a quantum physicist I know that all human knowledge is stored in the heightened energy states of fundamental particles who choose to live in brotherly harmony within tightly bound communities of deoxyribonucleic acid. I also know, from the work of Einstein, Rosen and Bose that these molecules can sometimes share experiences instantaneously, no matter how far apart they are. Intellectually I am forced to argue that the scope of the love demanded of a Mason is infinite. This is daunting, as it means that you must not only learn to love your fellow living creatures, and even all the living consciousnesses in the Universe (including the Great Architect, how ever you envisage He/She/It) but must also learn to love yourself.

The paradox of this task is that the less detail you know about an entity the easier it is to love it. Religious fanatics demonstrate this in the form of a self-consuming love for something which by its very nature is ultimately unknowable, yet the most extreme of these fanatics show no love for their fellow humans, let alone for themselves. This paradox of love is what forces me to suggest that the scope of Masonic Brotherly Love has to be infinite and extend to all manifestations of the life force including the life force within you. This implies learning to love yourself, perhaps the most challenging demand that Masonic Initiation has made on me.

In *The Ceremony of Initiation.- Analysis and Commentary*. [Watkins(1932)] Bro Walter Wilmshurst, our founding Master says:

"Only he can really serve and help another who has first discharged his duty to himself and made himself competent to serve. "Self-love (says Shakespeare) is not so vile a sin as self-neglect"; and there are many people who neglect to improve themselves, whilst fussily trying to improve others.

During my Masonic writings I have studiously avoided the subject of love, as I have always found it difficult to love myself. Then recently, one of the past masters of the lodge, who was aware of my interest and shortcomings in this aspect of Masonic fulfilment gave me a copy of a fascinating book which he felt might help me better understand the nature of Masonic love.

At first sight it is a strange book and not obviously Masonic. It by a neuron-scientist, Dr Jill Bolte Taylor, who had a stroke which seriously damaged and incapacitated the left side of her brain. But she never lost her ability to observe the different nature of the functions of her wounded brain. She was fortunate enough to recover and then wrote a full account of what it was like to live with only the right hand half of her brain working. In effect she lived as a totally right brained individual for a considerable period of time. During that time she lost the ability to speak, to read and to write, but not her ability to feel, to understand or to love. Now how does this help understand the nature of Brotherly Love? Let me speculate, brethren.

I have long known that the right and left hand halves of any individual's brain have different skills and personality traits. I wrote at length about this in *Turning the Hiram Key*, where I argued the view that one of the ways in which Masonic ritual works is by stilling our chattering, self-critical left brain personality in order to allow the Mason's consciousness to move under the control of the right brain. In that book I wrote about how it felt to experience a stilling of my left-brain personality by taking part in Masonic ritual.

When you sense the light of the centre you realize a great sense of control over what would otherwise be the whims of fate. You feel that you are not alone in the cosmos, and your life becomes part of an intelligible plan. You know that goodness can triumph, and even death has a purpose. This holds true whether there really is a deeper reality, or even if it is just a perception generated by an odd brain state. Either way, you realize that all religions and the gods they define are just ways of interpreting the transcendental bliss that mystics have known through the ages.

I went on to develop this idea in *The Secret Power of Masonic Symbols* where I wrote:

In your head there are two complete working brains. The left and right hemispheres of the human brain are both individually capable of keeping you alive and functioning even if the other side of your head were destroyed. You didn't have a spare brain fitted at birth, so that if you are injured you could continue to live. There is a more subtle purpose. You have an evolutionary advantage in having two cerebral hemispheres. If this wasn't so then humans would have evolved a less complex and less biologically demanding unified brain.

Your two hemispheres communicate via a structure called a corpus callosum which is a massive connecting cable made up of about 800 million neurons which link your hemispheres. During the later half of the twentieth century one radical treatment for epilepsy involved cutting this link and creating an individual with two disconnected brains. Roger Sperry studied these patients and discovered that the two hemispheres are different and have evolved for different purposes. He found that the right hemisphere loves symbols and metaphor, while the left hemisphere likes words. Many vertebrates and all birds have also evolved split brains. Evolutionary pressure has created a common solution to a shared problem, and that pressure is linked to the nature of consciousness.

Freemasonry encourages you to "know yourself". As Bro Walter Wilmshurst explained in *The Ceremony of Initiation.- Analysis and Commentary*.

The instruction in the Great Lights is to reveal to the Candidate the basic Law and Principles of all being; whilst that in the lesser ones constitutes his first lesson in the "knowledge of himself" and teaches him that those Principles exist also within his own soul and provide him with lights sufficient to shape it into perfection and bring himself into harmony with Cosmic Law.

I would not necessarily use the term "within his own soul" to describe the place where these principles are to be found. I would prefer the term "within his own brain", as science tells me that consciousness is a function of a living brain.

Consciousness fulfills two conflicting functions, best understood in terms of how our attention works. To carry out delicate tasks your brain needs to focus attention narrowly (say to pick up a grain of corn instead of the piece of stone that lies next to it) but at the same time it has to maintain a wide open field of attention so it remains aware of predators. If you can't concentrate you starve, and if you don't remain alert you get killed and eaten. The evolutionary answer to meet these conflicting requirements was two brains, a right brain taking a wide overview, using symbols to compress information about the nature of surrounding reality, and a left brain able to concentrate on fiddly tasks. These two different ways of paying attention has made us susceptible to the influence of symbols and also has developed a formidable talent for self-criticism in our left brain. But we are all descended from an unbroken line of ancestors whose brains could do both. (Otherwise they would have starved or been eaten long before they got old enough to breed your great-many-times-great-grandparents.) Over the past few years I have conducted interviews with various brain scientists and experts on consciousness and followed up the reading they suggested. This has led me to the conclusion that the locus of the transcendental expansion of cognizance which Bro Walter Wilmshurst called "awareness of the Centre" is located in the right brain.

But this could only be speculation without any independent evidence, apart from my own subjective experiences with lightning strikes, Masonic ritual and meditation. Now in this book by Jill Bolte Taylor (*My Stroke of Insight*) I was offered evidence that Freemasonry has learned how to teach its followers how to tap into the richness of right-brain modes of thought. Here is what Dr Bolte Taylor had to say the day after her stroke, when she awoke in hospital.

Despite my neurological trauma, an unforgettable sense of peace pervaded my entire being and I felt calm. Although I rejoiced in my perception of connection to all that is, I shuddered at the awareness that I was no longer a normal human being. How on earth would I exist as a member of the human race with this heightened perception that we are each a part of it all, and that the life force energy within each of us contains the power of the universe?

How could I fit in with our society when I walk the earth with no fear? I was, by anyone's standard, no longer normal. In my own unique way, I had become severely mentally ill. And I must say, there was both freedom and challenge for me in recognizing that our perception of the external world, and our relationship to it, is a product of our neurological circuitry. For all those years of my life, I really had been a figment of my own imagination!

Wasn't it interesting that although I could not walk or talk, understand language, read or write, or even roll my body over, I knew that I was okay? The now off-line intellectual mind of my left hemisphere no longer inhibited my innate awareness that I was the miraculous power of life. I knew I was different now - but never once did my right mind indicate that I was "less than" what I had been before. I was simply a being of light radiating life into the world. Regardless of whether or not I had a body or brain that could connect me to the world of others, I saw myself as a cellular masterpiece. In the absence of my left hemisphere's negative judgment, I perceived myself as perfect, whole, and beautiful just the way I was.

That final sentence reminded me of Bro Wilmshurst's teaching about the Third Degree, that in order to be open to the light of the centre you have to allow your ego to die. This is exactly what happened to Dr Bolte Taylor, the critical ego of her left brain died. Later, as she re-learned the power of speech (using what remained of her left brain) and was taught to read and write again she commented.

I realized that the blessing I had received from this experience was the knowledge that deep internal peace is accessible to anyone at any time. I believe the experience of Nirvana exists in the consciousness of our right hemisphere, and that at any moment, we can choose to hook into that part of our brain. With this awareness, I became excited about what a difference my recovery could make in the lives of others - not just those who were recovering from a brain trauma, but to everyone with a brain! I imagined the world filled with happy and peaceful people and I became motivated to endure the agony I would have to face in the name of recovery. My stroke of insight would be: peace is only a thought away, and all we have to do to access it is silence the voice of our dominating left mind. *[ie let our ego die]*

If I had to choose one word to describe the feeling I feel at the core of my right mind, I would have to say joy. My right mind is thrilled to be alive! I experience a feeling of awe when I consider that I am simultaneously capable of being at one with the universe, while having an individual identity whereby I move into the world and manifest positive change.

If you have lost your ability to experience joy, rest assured the circuitry is still there. It is simply being inhibited by more anxious and/or fearful circuitry. How I wish you could lose your emotional baggage, just like I did, and shift back into your natural state of joy! The secret to hooking into any of these peaceful states is the willingness to stop the cognitive loops of thought, worry, and any ideas that distract us from the kinesthetic and sensory experience of being in the here and now. Most important, however, our desire for peace must be stronger than our attachment to our misery, our ego, or our need to be right.

This little book, (*My Stroke of Insight*, Hodder, J Bolte Taylor, 2008) provides experimental evidence that the blissful state of mind which Bro. Wilmshurst taught was at the centre of Freemasonry, is within us all, and we can all learn how to access it.

Dr Bolte Taylor explains.

Prior to this experience with stroke, the cells in my left hemisphere had been capable of dominating the cells in my right hemisphere. The judging and analytical character in my left mind dominated my personality. When I experienced the hemorrhage and lost my left hemisphere language center cells that defined my self, those cells could no longer inhibit the cells in my right mind. As a result, I have gained a clear delineation of the two very distinct characters cohabiting my cranium. The two halves of my brain don't just perceive and think in different ways at a neurological level, but they demonstrate very different values based upon the types of information they perceive, and thus exhibit very different personalities. My stroke of insight is that at the core of my right hemisphere consciousness is a character that is directly connected to my feeling of deep inner peace. It is completely committed to the expression of peace, love, joy, and compassion in the world.

But she goes further writing about how her right brain was capable of a compassionate love which surprised her, once she managed to rebuild language circuits within her left brain and articulate the experience..

If I had to pick one output (action) word for my right mind, I would have to choose compassion.

Generally, most of us are compassionate with those we see as our equals. The less attached we are to our ego's inclination for superiority, the more generous of spirit we can be with others. When we are being compassionate, we consider another's circumstance with love rather than judgment. We see a homeless person or a psychotic person and approach them with an open heart, rather than fear, disgust, or aggression. Think about the last time you reached out to someone or something with genuine compassion.

To be compassionate is to move into the right here, right now with an open heart consciousness and a willingness to be supportive.

Freemasonry during the six hundred years it has spent studying the nature of immortal symbols and their interaction with the mind of mankind has developed ways of accessing that blissful, compassionate state of being. Work at you daily steps of Masonic knowledge and our Masonic Art will enable you to love your brethren, your world, your universe and yourself.

Essay 10 - Thoughts on a Black and White Pavement

At the Lodge of Living Stones we use what we call a "Dark Silence" both before and after our ceremonies. During that silence we turn off the electric lights, leaving only the flickering flames of the officers candles and eternal flame of the centre to make the form of the lodge visible in the darkness. In this dim glow all colour vision is suppressed and I can only see the silent, meditating lodge, in many shades of gray.

The purpose of the opening silence is to give the brethren an opportunity to still their chaotic thoughts and prepare their minds before the ritual work. The closing silence serves to allow a few moments of quiet reflection on the import of the ritual we have just worked or the lecture we have just listened to before we return to the hustle of the outside world.

Like every other Freemason's lodge the temple of the Lodge of Living Stones contains ornaments, furniture, and jewels. But the relative visibility of these features change during a dark silence. The furniture becomes dark amorphous masses and the jewels sink into the blackness. But the darkness serves to make the ornaments more visible.

At first, as the lights are lowered, the lodge seems to be quite black but as I concentrate on stilling the rush and chatter of thoughts I find that my eyes begin to adjust to the lower level of light. I become aware of the dark and silent figures of the brethren sitting around the perimeter of the lodge. I see the dim mass of the altar in the centre of the lodge, faintly lit from above by the flickering candle which symbolizes the eternal light of the centre. But as I sit in the darkness of meditation the most striking feature of the scene is the high contrast between the black and white squares of the beautiful pavement of the lodge flooring.

The black squares become blacker and white squares a dull grey. From where I sit, at the organ, in the north-east corner of the lodge I can see two patterns on the floor. If I look to the East I see a line of alternating black and white squares with each white square surrounded by black squares and each black square surrounded by white. I am reminded that in midst of the darkness of ignorance there is a light to be found, if only my mind can adjust learn to see it. Likewise I am reminded that when I think I am standing on a bright white square of understanding I am surrounded on all sides by things I do not yet understand. Shadows of ignorance surround each particle of knowledge that I take such pride in knowing.

But if I turn my eyes forty-five degrees to the right, so that I look across the centre of the lodge towards the south-east corner I see a different aspect of this beautiful flooring of the lodge. The squares of the flooring are transformed into diamond lozenges which march in straight undeviating lines from the North-West towards the South- East.

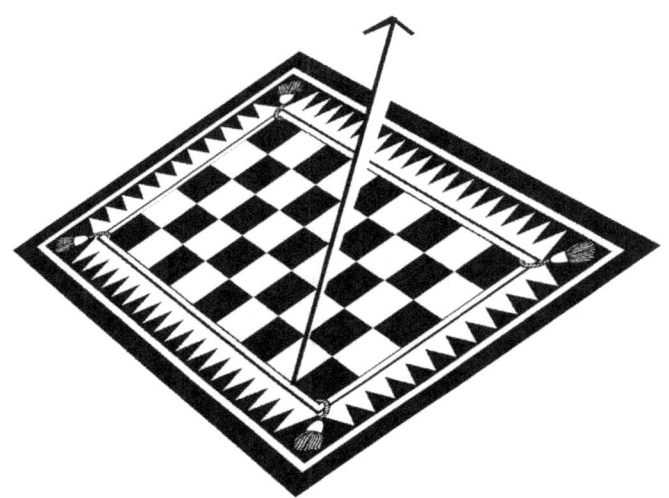

The symbolism is clear. If I can change my own viewpoint then I can move from the West towards the East on a clearly marked path which follows a white path of enlightened knowledge.

The strange thing about these two viewpoints is that as I try to still the thoughts of the day from my mind, I can only see one of these viewpoints at any moment. If I perceive the enclosed squares then I can not see the diagonal lines of lozenges leading to the East, but if I move my perception to see the lozenges then I cannot see the wall of black ignorance which surrounds each of the white squares. Like the familiar image of the Greek vase which flips to become two human faces, I can only see one viewpoint at once. As I try to still my mind I also try to hold both viewpoints in my vision but I never see both at once.

The ritual tells us that the Mosaic Pavement is the black and white flooring of the Lodge by reason of its being variegated and chequered. It points out the diversity of objects which decorate and adorn the creation, the animate as well as the inanimate parts thereof. The ritual goes to explain why the black and white mosaic work was introduced into Freemasonry saying that - the steps of man are trod in the various and uncertain incidents of life, and his days are variegated and chequered by a strange contrariety of events, his passage through this existence, though sometime attended by prosperous circumstances, is often beset by a multitude of evils; hence our Lodge is furnished with Mosaic work, to point out the uncertainty of all things here on earth.

Today I may travel in prosperity tomorrow I may totter on the uneven path of weakness, temptation, and adversity. Then while such emblems are before me, I am morally instructed not to boast of anything but to give heed to my ways, to walk up rightly and with humility before the Great Architect, as there is no station in life on which pride can be stably founded.

Some are born to more elevated situations than others, yet, when in the grave, we are all on the level, death destroys all distinctions; and while our feet tread on this Mosaic work, we should, as good men and Masons, practice charity, maintain harmony, and endeavour to live in unity and brotherly love.

When I reflect on the mosaic pavement I am attempting to see both darkness and light as one. But as I try to drive from my mind the thoughts of my daily work, no matter how hard I concentrate I cannot see both viewpoints of the black and white pavement simultaneously. As I explained previously one or the other flips into view. It is the effort of trying to see both views which stills the clamour of my thoughts and quietens my mind. As I prepare to engage in silent and intimate union with the ritual words of the ceremony my contemplation of the ambiguous pattern and discontinuous patterns of the black and white squares helps me still my rushing thoughts.

When the Master instructs that the lights are lowered it is to allow the darkness to fill our temple so that the splendour of daily light no longer distracts us from the silence symbolism of the path through darkness and light. The path we must find if we are to leave the West and journey to the East.

The paradox of my search for the light of the East, as represented by the black and white pavement, is that I must learn to embrace my dread of darkness and admit the black depths of my ignorance if I am to prepare myself to work with that love and harmony which is needed to bring into being that corporate entity which is the Perfect Lodge.

During the dark silence of preparation, I reflect on the ornaments of the lodge which the darkness makes visible. I learn to face my individual darkness to allow a new fragment of white shaped Truth to surround itself with shadow so that its brilliance will not dazzle me into incomprehension. Though this contemplation of my experience of light and darkness, of thought and feeling, I try to prepare myself to approach the portal to the holy mysteries of the Centre. I hope my reflections on the mysterious ambiguity of the black and white pavement may help you to use it in your own search for Truth.

Essay 11 - The Mystery of the Ashlars

Recently I was invited to visit a lodge in the heart of rural Yorkshire. I was extremely impressed with their rough ashlar. It was a magnificent chunk of millstone grit which had been crudely chiselled out of a cliff face and lugged into the lodge. It was not only impressive to look at it was also hard and heavy. (I know this because I managed to stub my toe on it whilst walking about the lodge to give a lecture.)

After the meeting, as I drove home, my sat-nav took me along a winding road up a hill. The road got narrower and twistier as it snaked ever upwards. Then I realized I was being guided across across the dark expanse of Ilkley Moor,

Its dark skies were impressive. I couldn't resist stopping my car to stand and marvel at the bright stars of the celestial canopy so piercingly cold above me. When I doused my car lights I couldn't see a single artificial light. I felt as tiny as a mote of dust as I stood beneath that sparkling dome of Eternity.

I knew that hidden within that encircling gloomy landscape there are a set of wonderfully worked stones, created by my ancient Yorkshire brethren to celebrate the perpetual lights of the Great Architect which slowly spiralled above the dark plateau of the moor. I thought of them hefting their crude hammer stones and antler bone chisels to cut the beautiful spirals and circles into the hard, knobbly stones. How little have the working tools of a Mason changed over the millennia since my ancient brethren had sweated to create beautifully worked stones to align with the raising and setting of the sun.

It was easy to see how the vast expense of cosmos, now clearly visible from the centre of Ilkley Moor, could have inspired them. But what passed through my mind, as I stood in that sparkling darkness, was how enduring is our human habit of cutting small chunks of stone from a rock strata, and reshaping them to use for symbolic purposes in our mental landscape.

Earlier that evening I had admired that rough block of uneven stone, hacked from the bedrock of this moor and placed before the junior warden's pedestal in the lodge. I had been taught to call it the rough ashlar. It had been introduced to me as the symbol of the soul of a newly made Mason before he has begun to work on shaping and refining himself.

This ancient practice of taking rough stones, working their surfaces before placing them in significant situations has been enacted in this part of Yorkshire for at least five thousands years. The decorated stones of Ilkley Moor, with so many circles and centres cut into them, stand witness to this need humans have to shape stones. It is a way of facing up to our own mortality whilst making something for our ideas to speak beyond the grave to generations as yet unborn. This is a practice we Freemasons have refined to a Royal Art.

Our rough ashlar is an uncouth, uncut stone, roughly wrenched from the rock wall of the quarry. It represents the soul of the newly made Entered Apprentice. It is rough and unhewn but the application of industry and ingenuity by Masonically trained workmen can reshape it. The apprentice is given three tools to help him shape it into due form, and render it fit to take its place in more complex structure.

This irregular stone represents the soul of man in his infant or primitive state. It is rough and unpolished until under the kind care and attention of a liberal and virtuous system of education, his mind becomes cultivated. So is he rendered a fit member of civilized society.

The apprentice who desires to rise to the heights that his own being is capable of, must first crush his lower nature and inclinations. He must perfect his conduct, by struggles against his own natural propensities. His base material nature is symbolized by the rough ashlar, crude and unpolished as it is dragged from the clay of the quarry. He must use spiritual tools to hack, shape and polish the rough ashlar of his own nature into the perfect cube of an enlightened soul.

The spiritual tools he is given to use on the surface of the rough stone are the chisel and gavel. We show a steel chisel and wooden gavel. But its function has not changed from the antler bone chisel and rough hammer stones of the Ilkley Moor rock carvers. The chisel still concentrates the diffused force of the gavel into a cutting edge and enables it to remove all knobs and excrescences which mar the smooth surface the craftsman is trying to reveal to the world. It represents the power of education to change and improve the individual.

This common Gavel represents the force of our conscience, which keeps down all vain and unbecoming thoughts which might otherwise obtrude into our thoughts and pollute our words and actions. As we gain skill in the use of this tool, it becomes a Master's gavel that can control the Lodge. Its knocks can create order and obedience within the Lodge. And as the lodge is but a symbol of the Mason's soul, so we see how the gavel can be used to knock it into a better shape.

As a Mason you learn that your body and soul, are the level ground upon which you must try to build an altar to represent your spiritual life. You are encouraged to allow no debasing habit of thought or conduct, to defile this work. As an apprentice Mason you are given the common wooden gavel to help you smooth the rough ashlar of your imperfect soul and shape it to towards the perfect symbol of a cubical altar to stand at the centre of your consciousness. You are encouraged to use the force of conscience to control your anger and intolerance. And the better craftsman you become the more the shape of your soul morphs towards that of a perfect ashlar.

The ritual tells us that the perfect ashlar is for the experienced craftsman to try, and adjust, his jewels on. It is a true die or perfect square, fit to be tried by the Square and Compasses. It represents the soul of a Mason after a regular well-spent life in acts of piety and virtue. He can only be tried and approved by the Square of TGAOU and the Compass of his own self-convincing conscience.

To attain the state of spiritual development signified by the Perfect Ashlar (which is the work of the Masonic Second Degree), you need to bring your soul and body into a balanced relationship. Then you are ready to pass through the crucial regenerative experience known as the cross, or transition from natural to supranatural life. So this perfect ashlar ashlar symbolizes a state of balance and harmony which is the goal of every Fellowcraft Freemason.

But the cube of the perfect ashlar contains a further secret. Unfolded, it denotes and takes the form of the cross of four right angles or squares. These make up the angle of 360 degrees which subscribe a circle.

The cross as a philosophical symbol long pre-dates Christianity It is significant in Freemasonry as a symbol of the four primordial elements (fire, water, air, earth) brought together into a state of balanced harmony. All newly made Masons have too much or too little of one or the other of these elements in their composition. To restore their inner elements of the body, mind, spirit and soul to balance and harmony is the life-problem we all share with them. The cross of the unfolded (or developed) perfect ashlar is a conspicuous symbol of the human soul. Our ego is bound by the cross of the four material elements which it must subdue into balance and harmony, As the ritual says we must "make all our passions and prejudices coincide with the strict line of virtue and in every pursuit to have eternity in view". By unfolding the perfect ashlar we see that the angles of the circle contain the Divine Spark of our own soul.

But the perfect ashlar of the balanced soul is not just a metaphor, it is also building block. To understand its greater purpose we need to consider the structures we might construct from it. It might become a building block of a great temple or a part of an altar.

The altar is a double cube, worked from two cubical smooth ashlars into a perfect six-sided form. It is a symbol of what your mind can become if you can make it perfect in all its parts. Its concealed underside, resting on the Earth, stands for the hidden submerged depths of your subconscious. Its four sides facing the four quarters of the Lodge signify your human elementary nature brought into a balance as a harmonious four-square foundation stone for a spiritual building. Its upper side is exposed to the light of the bright morning star. On its surface rest the three great lights of Masonry. It is the reverse of the concealed underside. It represents the consciousness of a purified personality turning away from mundane interests and facing towards the source of light. From this altar a ladder of innumerable steps leads to the firmament and thence to infinity.

You are striving to be not only the altar made from the hard stones of the earth, but also the builder of it, the offering upon it and the priest who serves it. Only then are you ready to ascend the great spiritual ladder and achieve union with the centre beyond the heavens.

Refined ashlars can be used to build the altar which can now be seen to symbolize the personality of brethren working together and "made perfect in all their parts." The completed altar is a double cube with a six-sided form. The four sides facing the quarters of the lodge symbolize Masonic souls moulded into a balanced, harmonious four square foundation for loftier work. The exposed upper side supports the three great emblematic lights. It represents the corporate consciousness of the Perfect Lodge turned towards the heights in aspiration for union with the source of light. And it reminds us that only by building on the work of our Masonic predecessors can we create this extended symbol. The lower side reminds us that we are all hewn from the same quarry.

The rough ashlar can only be squared and perfected by chipping and polishing. You learn that difficulty, adversity and persecution serve a useful purpose. These hardships are your wages and you must learn to accept them "without scruple and without diffidence", knowing that you are justly entitled to them, and from the confidence you have in the integrity of your Employer in the grand purpose of creating eternity, the GAOTU.

When you set your feet upon the path to the light of the East; when you seek to pass between the pillars and enter deeper knowledge; when you mount the winding stairway to the heights; you make a break with your past and put your old methods of life behind you. You detach yourself from the interests you previously prized, in favour of something better. You will find yourself moved between states of light and joy, and periods of darkness and dismay. You will doubt the path you have set yourself upon. Experiences such as this constitute the "wages". The fact they are being paid is evidence of spiritual progress. If you remain stagnated in your old unregenerate life you are spiritually asleep. But as you awake from your torpor you stir up adverse energies. These experiences are salutary lessons in wisdom and conducive to that stability of soul which you are working to perfect.

We *can* change ourselves from a rough ashlar to a perfect cube, and be carried from natural darkness into supernatural light by being lifted on the efforts of our corporate lodge. Just as the outer body can be opened for surgical investigation, so the Lodge can be opened to help us understand the mechanism and purpose of our inner self. The spirit indwells the mind, just as the mind suffuses the body; but only in the mind, once it is rectified, purified and worked, from the rough ashlar to the perfect cube, can the Centre be brought to life and consciousness. So can the perfect cube be unfolded to reveal the angles of the circle of which we are the centre.

When you first join a lodge your soul is thought of as a rough stone freshly hacked from the living rock of the quarries. It has a coarse and crude aspect, yet within it there is a perfect cube of polished stone. You are given tools to work on your soul and are encouraged to make daily progress in shaping yourself into a perfected state. You are urged to control your base urges so that your soul may become more regular in shape, You are encouraged to develop your mind that you might acquire the polish of a liberal education and above all you are urged to behave honestly and fairly, to treat all society in a square and honest way, until you become a perfect square in all your aspects, so your soul reveals the hidden shape of a perfect square in all three dimensions.

But brethren, Freemasonry does not deal with the material building-work of any outward structure, but with the disordered temple of the human soul. Its rituals symbolize something deep and personal, the shaping of your Mason's soul from the rough ashlar into the perfect cube.

As I stood in the dark silence of Ilkley Moor and looked up towards that ancient light falling from the bright stars of the Cosmos I realized I was looking deep into the quarry of the GAOTU. Those bright points in the heavens had created all the atoms, molecules and matter of my body and now, by utilizing the mental tools of the Craft. I was trying to shape that dancing pattern of molecules into that immaterial awareness I can call my soul.

Essay 12 - How does a Mason Progress?

In the lecture of the First Degree the ritual tells us that we should "learn to rule and subdue our passions, and make a further progress in Masonry," but it doesn't say what form that progress should take.

The preamble to the lecture of the Second degree says that "Masonry is a progressive science consisting of different Degrees, calculated for the more gradual advancement in the knowledge of its mysteries; according to the progress we make, we limit or extend our inquiries, and in proportion to our capacities, we attain to a greater or lesser degree of perfection." But what are the mysteries we are intended to inquire about? The charge of this degree says

Masonry being a progressive science, when you were made an Entered Apprentice you were placed at the North East part of the Lodge, to show that you were newly admitted; you are now placed at the South East part, to mark the progress you have made in the science; you now stand, to all external appearance, a just and upright Fellow Craft Freemason, and I give it you in strong terms of recommendation ever to continue, and act as such; and, as I trust the import of the former charge neither is, nor ever will be, effaced from your memory, I shall content myself with observing, that as in the previous degree you made yourself acquainted with the principles of moral truth and virtue, you are now permitted to extend your researches into the hidden mysteries of nature and science.

The final degree lecture spreads some light on the matter saying

Every degree of Masonry is progressive, and cannot be attained but by time, patience, and assiduity. In the First Degree, we are taught the duties we owe to God, to our neighbour, and to ourselves. In the Second Degree, we are admitted to participate in the mysteries of human science, and to trace the goodness and majesty of the Creator, by minutely analyzing His works. But the Third Degree is the cement of the whole; it is calculated to bind men together by mystic points of fellowship, as in a bond of fraternal affection and brotherly love; it points to the darkness of death and to the obscurity of the grave as the forerunner of a more brilliant light, which shall follow at the resurrection of the just, when these mortal bodies which have been long slumbering in the dust shall be awakened, reunited to their kindred spirit, and clothed with immortality.

So now the object of Masonic progress become clear. It is to understand and become a part of the kindred spirit of mankind and the key to that kindred spirit which activates mankind is the individual self. So to make progress a Mason must learn about himself and then about how he relates others. But how does he do this, and what is the self?

The clue is in progression. To understand something fully you need to appreciate it from all possible aspects. This is the meaning and purpose of Masonic progression. You begin as a Candidate, and things are done to you, then you move up the chain of officers and do things to others. Only when you have played every role can you see every aspect. You have been symbolically killed and you have symbolically killed another, you have symbolically died and have attended your own funeral, you have been raised and also raised a brother. But how does such a complex and progressive ritual help you to know yourself? Let me begin by speculating about the nature of self, I see the concept of self as fivefold and all five points of self need to present.

1. Continuity: There must be a sense of continuity about your concept of yourself. It must seem that the person who went to sleep is the same person who wakes up. There must be an unbroken thread running through the whole of your existence so you can appreciate past, present and future.

2. Unification: The must be a coherence to your concept of self. You may experience a wide range of memories,

sensory experiences, thoughts and beliefs but you must feel a unifying force within your idea of self which makes sense of all the various inputs.

3. Control: You must have a sense of ownership and control over your self. You have to feel that you have a home within your own body and it does what you ask it to do, when you ask it to.

4. Freewill: You must have a sense of freewill or choice which places you in charge of your own actions. You can wriggle your own fingers anytime you want, but you cannot wriggle mine. If you feel your actions to be forced on you by outside forces then you lose your sense of self.

5. Reflection: You must have the capacity for reflection. A self that is not self aware is not a self at all.

The regular practice of Masonic rituals reinforces each of these defining attributes of the self. The progression and repeatability of the ritual gives continuity. The range of degrees and lectures provides unification. The order and calm of the lodge gives control to the presiding officers. The choices offered by the questions put to the Candidate illustrates freewill, The dark silences and the discussion after the ceremony provides material for reflection. So one way to progress is to study, practice and work the rituals. But is that enough to make progress?

Progress in the study and development of our self has to be a way of reshaping and moulding the structures of our brains. Our brains as essentially model-making machines where we construct from the input of our senses a virtual reality simulation of the world about us. Within this construct we also need to create model's of other people's minds so that we can empathize and interact with them. We need to understand the motivation of others so we can respond to them appropriately. And we need to know how we respond with our secret self. Study of the book of the Perfect Lodge can help here as it provides just such a two fold model. The Lodge can been seen as a co-operating community which works together to achieve corporate understanding and also as a model of the various impulses, forces and stimuli which work within us to push us to act. From this contemplation we learn empathy and from the imitation involved in working ritual we learn to grow and develop. The quality of imitation is perhaps the most powerful evolutionary force at our disposal. By learning to imitate we can leapfrog from the slow pace of Darwinian evolution into the fast track of Lamarckian transition.

Finally Freemasonry encourages the development of the practice of Free Will, which is a defining quality of the human self. It is the first lesson the ritual teaches as we are first announced:

Mr A.B., a poor candidate, in a state of darkness, who has been well and worthily recommended, regularly proposed and approved in open Lodge and now comes of his own free will and accord, properly prepared, humbly soliciting to be admitted to the mysteries. and privileges. of Freemasonry.

And the issue is revisited in the obligation we take before becoming a Master Mason which begins:

I, A. B., in the presence of the Most High, and of this worthy and worshipful Lodge of Master Masons, duly constituted, regularly assembled, and properly dedicated, of my own free will and accord do hereby

But how does the meeting, working with, and discussing with, Freemasons encourage the development of Free Will? It was demonstrated some time ago by the experiments of Liber and Kornhuber that the voluntary decision to wriggle a finger was preceded, some 750 milli-secs before the movement by a readiness potential, even though their subjects recorded that their finger moved the moment they decided to move it. Yet there is almost a full second's activity taking place in the brain before the free will action kicks in. So do you really have Free Will or is your subconscious working the conscious self like a puppet on a string of neurons? And what is the evolutionary explanation for this strange finding? It seems that natural selection has deliberately selected for brains which have a built in neural delay so that the subjective sensation of free will decisions is delayed to coincide, not with the onset of brain commands but, with their actual execution. This is not the case with subconscious reflex actions. We pull our hand out of the fire before our self is even aware of the danger. The autonomous emotional system handles those sort of incidents and it is the impact of our emotional response which the first degree helps us learn to control. So the second degree is about training this delayed, slow reacting self-willed system to work in closer union with the quick responding autonomous systems which make up the bulk of our brain activity. The result of this ritual and reflection is to encourage these two brain systems to work more closely together and so help us achieve greater harmony within ourselves. But what about our interactions with others?

Humans need a nurturing culture to develop our more advanced mental functions. Children brought up by wolves never learn to speak, let alone how to construct mental models of their self-awareness. Freemasonry and its teachings provide an ideal nurturing culture for developing and reflecting on the nature of self-awareness. To return to the summary of progression given in the lecture of the third degree. The first degree we experience wide swings of instant acting raw emotion and learn how to handle it, in the second degree we learn how to develop our slow-acting mental agility and observational skill and only then, in the third degree are we forced to face up to the mortality of this self, which its own sense of continuity makes feel immortal. We have to learn how to die, and with this knowledge of the inevitability of death, which is so hard for a continuous-controlling self to understand, we become aware that our time to develop is limited. We are warned:

Be careful to perform your allotted task while it is yet day; listen to the voice of nature which bears witness that, even in this perishable frame, there resides a vital and immortal principle, which inspires a holy confidence, that the Lord of Life will enable us to trample the King of Terrors beneath our feet, and lift our eyes to that bright morning star whose rising brings peace and tranquillity to the faithful and obedient of the human race.

Essay 13 – Wilmshurst - A Symbolic Summary of the Craft - the Tracing Board of the Centre

After fifty years of studying Freemasonry Bro. Walter Wilmshurst decided that Freemasonry teaches that a human is made up of four segments, each forming a fourth part of a circle. The circle represents the totality of being which a Master of the Craft will try to balance in all its parts. When this is achieved the spirit becomes a complete and rounded whole with its focus on the centre, and only when this balance is achieved can the light at the centre be seen. He wrote that 'each daily step in Masonic knowledge should help us develop our Masonic skill, so that we grow in our ability to perceive this great light and harmony which lies at the centre of our being'. Only when we learn to perceive 'the light unquenchable' within our own mind, do we become a Master Mason.

To help his brethren follow this path Bro. Walter used a private tracing-board to instruct the senior members of his lodge. Bro. Douglas Inglesent, the then librarian of the Lodge of Living Stones found a copy of this board, marked "Private not to be Retained" and initialed by Bro. Walter among Wilmshurst's papers

Bro. Walter did not leave a written explanation of the board but in this essay I have drawn on all his writings to reconstruct his thoughts on the symbols it shows.

The tracing board is set with the boundaries of the lodge, and its purpose is to draw attention to the four symbolic directions. East, West, South and North. The symbolism of these directions is a theme, which Wilmshurst returns to often, so I will summarize his ideas. . I reproduce this tracing-board of the centre below.

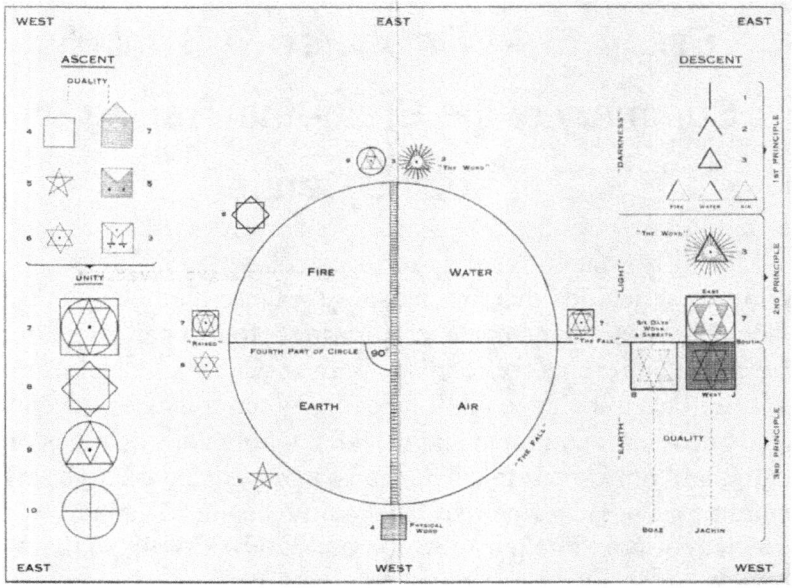

The main direction of the Tracing board runs from East at the top to West at the bottom. This is no accident as Wilmshurst sees the transition from East to West as vitally important. He says:

Our Ritual, after explaining the cultural purpose and discipline of the first two Degrees, goes on to say 'Masonry finally teaches you how to die'. This involves something deep. The Craft prescribes for its followers a technique of *living,* so why does its ritual speak of a definite technique of *dying?* Is this a secret science of the process of mystical death and resurrection, which qualifies candidates to learn?

Wilmshurst said it is a delicate and deeply concealed subject, never openly discussed and only to be learned from the private instruction of the Master to whom a Candidate is affiliated, hence his use of this private tracing-board. He goes on to say.

The Ritual hints at this secret technique. Most unenlightened people dread death in any form and wish to hear as little of it as they can. But Wilmshurst insists is that it is a mystical dying that results in "raising" and makes a Candidate an Initiate. The aspirant "suffers a sea change, into something rich and strange." This change is an inward, transforming consciousness by a literal "renewing" of the mind.

It does not change your outward appearance. You return to the "companions of your former toils" and resume your usual activities. Yet your whole being is "raised" to a higher power and reinforced by life of a higher quality and voltage. This was once called being "made perfect". "To be perfect is to be initiated" was an old saying, and in Greek the same word was used for both "perfection" and "initiation."

But to return to the four quarters of the lodge. The North is the side of un-enlightenment, the place of darkness. It calls for exertion in the teeth of opposition. It presents darkness and difficulty that call forth the energy of the spirit. The North is associated with mental darkness and signifies the place of imperfection and un-development. Wilmshurst notes that in olden times the bodies of suicides, reprobates and unbaptized children were always buried in the north or sunless side of a churchyard.

Junior members of the Craft are seated in the north, for, symbolically, it represents the condition of the spiritually unenlightened, the novice whose spiritual latent light has not yet risen above the horizon of consciousness to disperse the clouds of material interests and the impulses of the sensual life.

The East of the Lodge represents spirituality, the highest and most sacred mode of consciousness. Often this is little developed but is still latent and becomes active in moments of stress or deep emotion.

The West, the polar opposite of the East, represents normal rational understanding, the consciousness we employ in every-day affairs. It is material-mindedness or common sense. Midway between East and West is the South, the meeting-place of spiritual intuition and rational understanding. It is a point denoting abstract thought and intellectual power at its highest. Opposite this is the North, a sphere of benightedness and ignorance, controlled by sense-reactions and impressions received by our lowest and least reliable mode of perception, our physical senses.

Thus the four sides of the Lodge point to four different, yet progressive, modes of consciousness. These are sense-impression (North), reason (West), intellectual idealization (South), and spiritual intuition (East), making up four possible ways of knowing.

According to your development and education you tend to employ only the first two or perhaps three of these. This limitation on your outlook on life means that your knowledge of truth is restricted and imperfect. Full and perfect knowledge is possible only when the deep-seeing vision and consciousness of your spiritual principle has been awakened and added to your other cognitive faculties. This is possible only to the true Master, with all four methods of knowledge in perfect balance and adjusted like the four sides of the Lodge. This is why the Master and Past-Masters are placed in the East.

The personality of the Mason is made up of four basic metaphysical elements called by the ancients fire, water, air and earth. In the Tracing Board this is represented a circle made of up four equal parts. The four-sidedness of this circle is a reminder that the human organism is compounded of those four elements in balanced proportions. Water represents the psychic nature; Air, the mentality, Fire, the will and nervous force; whilst Earth is the condensation in which the other three become stabilized and encased.

The circle in the centre of the tracing board represents our personal temple and within it are four right angles, each forming the fourth part of the circle of our self.

In the north-west is the earthly body which concentrates on the irrational demands of the flesh. It is represented by the element Earth.

The south-west is the rational mind which can control and counterpoise the irrational body. It is represented by Air.

The south-east quarter is the emotional or psychic mind which can be swayed by both rational and irrational elements and will be influenced by which ever is allowed to predominate. It is represented by the element Water.

The north east quarter is the spirit, a supra-rational principle which is capable of comprehending the transcendental nature of the unifying principle of the universe. It is shown as the element of Fire.

This diagram helps us to understand the purpose of the three degrees of the Craft. The First degree equips us to develop a rational mind and bring our intellect (Air in the tracing board) into balance with the irrational urges of the flesh (shown as Earth in the tracing board). To aid us in this we are equipped with postures, a lodge structure to focus our thinking and a set of symbols and spiritual tools. Only when we have balanced our rational mind against our bodily urges, learned how to how to use posture, to comprehend symbolism and gained proficiency in the use of spiritual tools are we ready to move on the Second degree.

The Second degree helps us to balance our intellect (Air) and our emotions (Water) so that we learn how to recognize truth and discriminate between irrational urges of the flesh (Earth) and the truth of the spirit (Fire). We are given further postures, tools and symbols to help us strengthen our rational mind and learn to handle our emotions so that we are prepared for the discovery of the blazing star of truth, which is as yet only visible as darkness at our centre. Here we meet the spiral symbol, which can teach us how to approach the centre. The postures affect our body and feed back hormonal responses into our rational minds so helping us learn how to subdue emotion. But before we can proceed to the Third degree we must be prepared to let go of our ego and self-regard.

In the Third degree we allow our ego and rational mind to die so that our spirit may be reborn as the keystone of our being and be supported in its quest to attain the vision of light that emanates from the centre. The ritual of death and rebirth stills the urges of our body, our intellect and our emotion and brings forth the suppressed spirit. In this degree the circle of our being is rendered complete and perfect by acquiring mastery over its four component parts. When this is fully achieved a master of the craft has undergone a radical transformation of the mind and a regeneration of his entire nature. Now are we ready to allow the light of the centre to flow through fresh channels in the brain such that the true secret of the Craft may be internalized.

In the ritual of the Third Degree this is symbolized as the gates of will, intellect, and feelings respectively. At each entrance stands an aspect of our lower self, each a traitor, seeking the secrets of the spirit for selfish ends. An intuition of right conduct arises in the Initiates spirit and attempts to escape through the southern *gate of will*. Our lower self, afraid that it must reform its bad habits and prune its excesses, refuses let our spirit rise free.

Now our inner wisdom tries to escape through the northern *gate of intellect*. Here another aspect of the lower self resents it, afraid of the need to make fresh mental adjustments. Once more our spirit is struck down.

Finally this higher self staggers to the eastern *gate of feeling,* where all inspiration of spiritual vitality is stifled by our lower sensual nature. Our spirit, finding that its retreat cut off at the only three gates it knows from the outer life of the world, is slain and must await the master light of all our seeing. We must learn to discipline those three ruffians enlisting the principal officers in our personal lodge. Then, as Hiram Abif we are raised to become a balanced and harmonious personality, with the Blazing Star at our centre controlling all aspects of our life.

Wilmshurst calls this state of initiation the fifth kingdom of nature. He says that we should recognize it as a transcendental condition of consciousness. It is within you, not *of* this world yet personally realizable here and now. It is a treasure hidden in everyone's personal organism towards which all Masons should constantly aspire.

It is not a matter of time or place but of consciousness. He says that it comes as lightning coming from East to West, noting that these in the Masonic sense are our spiritual and material poles. The East represents Spirituality and the West Material and Rational thinking. The tension between them is implied by placing the symbolic eternal flame in the Centre of the Lodge to represent the light of consciousness.

The awareness of this state of consciousness is a change, which can be experienced in Initiation. When it happens it is a solemn crisis of psychological expansion which Wilmshurst says feels like a rending of one's mental veil, the subjectively heard ripping and crashing, like "the sound of a trumpet," of the delicate nerve webbing which hitherto has shut off perception from super sensual things, and finally the blinding blaze of light immortal which makes a man an Initiate.

The initiate placed in the N.E. corner is intended to see that on the one side of him is the path that leads to the perpetual light of the East, into which he is encouraged to proceed, and that on the other is that of spiritual obscurity and ignorance into which it is possible for him to remain or relapse. It is a parable of the dual paths of life open to each one of us; on the one hand the path of selfishness, material desires and sensual indulgence, of intellectual blindness and moral stagnation; on the other the path of moral and spiritual progress, in pursuing which one may decorate and adorn the Lodge within him with the ornaments and jewels of grace and with the invaluable furniture of true knowledge, and which he may dedicate, in all his actions, to the service of God and of his fellow men. And mark that of those jewels some are said to be moveable and transferable, because when displayed in our own lives and natures their influence becomes transferred and communicated to others and helps to uplift and sweeten the lives of our fellows; whilst some are immoveable because they are permanently fixed and planted in the roots of our own being, and are indeed the raw material which has been entrusted to us to work out of chaos and roughness into due and true form.

The lodge is shown as an oblongated (or duplicated) square because man's organism does not consist of his physical body alone. The physical body has its "double" or ethereal counterpart in the astral body which is an extension of the physical nature and compound of the same four elements in an impalpable and more tenuous form. The oblong spatial form of the Lodge must therefore be considered as referable to the physical and ethereal nature in each of us.

During the rituals the candidate follows a path of spiral pilgrimage around the circumference of the circle, which contains the self. This path is described in terms of a sequence of symbols. Inspiration begins in the East with an upward facing equilateral triangle with a blazing light at its centre. This represents the rising of the bright morning star within the earth-based triangle of rational thought. The base of the triangle is aligned along the balance between the emotions and the intellect. (Earth-Air) whilst it apex points towards the spiritual East. It suggests that there is a spiritual star shining at the centre of the rational and emotional urges of the candidate.

The path continues to the south, the area of intellect. Here there is a more complex symbol consisting of a square, a circle, two interlaced equilateral triangles and a centre. The triangle can be drawn with the apex pointing upwards or downwards. These were known in medieval Kabbalism as the triangles of fire and water respectively. Symbolically the triangle of fire refers to the spiritual nature, and the triangle of water to the mental or rational nature. Wilmshurst says that one meaning of the interlaced triangles is when the spirit is in perfect balance with the mind. He goes on to state that the square, triangle, circle, and point, are symbols known as the "Platonic solids," i.e., the basic geometrical principles of the invisible Real and Eternal World that lies behind and controls the phenomenal and temporal world. This science of spiritual geometry reveals the true principles upon which our personal temple must be built.

The Square is the symbol of the human spirit as it is generated out of the inspiration, which underlies it. That spirit was created "square" and perfect though invested with freedom of choice and capacity for error.

But this symbol also has a circle with a centre point, within a square. The circle within a square has special significance. The square represents the spirit as it exists in the outward Universe, symbolized by the lodge with its directions and their significances. As the candidate moves around the circumference he is searching for the light of inspiration which initiated his quest. If he can make contact with that central principle by a voluntary renunciation of the intervening obstructions and inharmonious elements in himself, then he ceases to be a rationalized animal and becomes aware of omniscience. In this way he recovers the lost and genuine secrets of his own being as he reaches a point from which no Master Mason can ever err which it is the end, object and goal of his search.

The opening and closing of the Lodge in the Third Degree reveals the philosophy of the Masonic system. It says that the human spirit originated in the eternal East, in the world of Spirituality and not to any geographical direction - and that thence it has directed its course towards the West - the material world which is the antipodes of the spiritual. Its purpose in journeying from spiritual to physical conditions is a quest to recover something it has lost, but which by its own industry and suitable instruction it hopes to find. What it is that has been lost is not explicitly declared, but is implied and is stated to be the genuine secrets of a Master Mason. It is the loss of the essence of our own being. In other words the spirit has ceased to be aware of the cosmos and has degenerated into a limited terrestrial consciousness.

The square symbolized the influence of the outside cosmos that evolved this searching spirit. The circle was used by the old Initiates to demonstrate the microcosmic and all comprehensive nature of man. This symbol shows the candidate simultaneously as a square, finite, material and form-fettered, and yet as potentially a circle, — spiritual, infinite and free. It indicates that when his outward temporal self attains balance with his inward immortal spirit, the square of the former becoming equal to, and in equilibrium with, the circle of the latter his evolution is complete; he has wrought the purpose of that which made him man. He must gradually digest the Masonic teaching in the closed circle of his own mind to extracts its final values. When he does he will square the circle. This is an occult expression signifying that the deity, symbolized by the all-containing circle, has attained form and manifestation in a square or human spirit. It expresses the mystery of Initiation within the individual spirit.

But inside this symbol is a triangle with its apex downwards and base upwards, which is an ancient symbol of the psychic constitution known as the water triangle. It is interlaced with a fire triangle, a symbol of the spirit that imparts functional energy. Of itself the spirit would be passive, a negative quantity unbalanced by a positive opposite. Its active properties are the product of its union with an underlying and inspiring basis, modified by the good or evil tendencies of the personality. So by the interaction of the individual qualities of the personality, represented by the interlaced triangles the spirit may hope to find the glory at the centre within the square creation of the cosmos. And this symbol is first encountered in the southern part of the lodge, the area dominated by logic and learning. It is also found on the cusp point where the religious inclinations of the spirit (symbolized by water) meet the rational arguments of the material mind (symbolized by air).

Here is the point where the Masonic pilgrim is forced to rationalize his longing for spiritual understanding. What does he seek? What are the lost secrets he hopes will lead him to the the brightness of the centre, which he first glimpsed dimly through the imbalance of his emotions and rational mind. To find answers he must move on towards the west. The point where his emotions and reason will come into intimate contact with one another in the most material region of the lodge.

The symbol you meet at this point is a square, but a dark, black and threatening square. What does it mean? You are now deep in the work of the 2nd Degree — the education, discipline and control of your mental faculties, the gradual discovery of the secrets and mysteries of nature and of yourself as part of nature. You are trying to turn yourself into a true die or square. At this point your individualization as a unitary Ego attains its climax. The Perfect Cube represents man brought to perfection in the natural order. But perfection in the natural order is not your final goal. It is only a halfway house to the spiritual or ultra-natural order. It is where, when the Perfect Ashlar stage has been reached, there awaits for everyone the last and greatest trial, the death prefigured by our 3rd Degree, involving the annihilation of all sense of the personal self, the killing of the strongly individualized Ego-consciousness. The darkness of this square is that of death itself. This is the valley of death that our ritual tells us we need to travel towards if we are to rise and shine as the stars forever. And the first star is visible in the fading light of the south-western corner of the lodge.

As in the outer heavens of nature the sun, moon and stars exist and function, so in the personal heavens of man there operate metaphysical forces inherent in himself and described by the same terms. In the make-up of each of us exists a psychic magnetic field of various forces, determining our individual temperaments and tendencies and influencing our future. To those forces have also been given the names of sun, moon and planets, and the science of their interaction and outworking was the ancient science of astronomy, or, as it is now more often called astrology, which is one of the liberal arts and sciences recommended to the study of every Mason and the pursuit of which belongs in particular to the Fellowcraft stage. Now we are prepared for our first meeting with the five pointed star as it sets in west.

To become initiated involves dying; not a physical death, but a moral way of dying in which the spirit is loosened from the body and the sensitive life, and becomes temporarily detached and free to enter a world of Eternal Light. This, after drastic preliminary disciplines, was historically achieved in a state of trance and under the supervision of duly qualified Masters and Adepts who intromitted the candidate's liberated spirit into its own interior principles until it reached the Blazing Star or Glory at its own centre. In that light it simultaneously knew itself and God, and realized their unity and the points of fellowship between them. The five pointed star, represents meanings that will either disclose themselves to advancing experience or be imparted privately by a teacher to properly prepared pupils. To reach the glory of the centre we must be ready to let our Ego die. Wilmshurst warns that this is a dangerous process unless it is undertaken at that critical moment when the light of the bright morning star is about to rise in the our night sky.

To a candidate of strong virtue and level-headedness, who knows beforehand what he is doing and acts under a competent teacher, there is no danger in venturing into the hidden paths. He will act, and with safety, upon the age-old enjoinder of the Mysteries: To know; to will; to dare; and be silent.

Five *upward* steps lead from the First to the Second Degree. That is why we are told to lift our eyes to a bright five-pointed star whose rising in ourselves brings peace and salvation. From this symbol it is possible to develop five points of fellowship and self-identification.

The geometrical symbolist would think of the five kingdoms in terms of the point, the line, the square, the cube, and finally the pentagon or five-pointed star), each new kingdom involving an extra dimension of consciousness.

All things in Nature, then, shape towards a fifth kingdom. But understand this important truth; every kingdom is self-contained, shut off as it were by closed bulkheads; their bounds are set through which we cannot pass, and no leap from a lower to a higher kingdom is possible save on one condition, a previous death to the kingdom below it. No biologist can trace the point where decaying rock gives way to the minute lichen springing from it; nor the point where vegetable food becomes animal tissue, nor where sensory tissue permits the miraculous birth of human intelligence. This transition is not physically demonstrable as it is not a physical change, it occurs on subtle or subjective levels, at the interval or gap between the rungs of our symbolic ladder. All we know is that a change occurs, that a death of something precedes every new and higher begetting. And so it is when a man aspires to pass from the merely human to the Initiate degree of life; a death is involved, a death signified by our Third Degree. Such a death was always the culminating feature of the Ancient Mysteries and remains so with us. When our Ritual, after explaining the cultural purpose and discipline of the first two Degrees, goes on to say Masonry finally teaches you how to die, something much deeper is involved than meets the casual ear. The phrase veils the fact that, just as the Craft prescribes for aspirants a definite technique of *living,* so too it prescribes a definite technique of *dying,* a secret science of the process of mystical death and resurrection, which qualified candidates can come to learn. This is a delicate and deeply concealed subject, never openly discussed and only to be learned from the private instruction of the Master to whom the Candidate is affiliated. Our Ritual only gives a bare hint of it for the benefit of the perspicacious. The unenlightened man dreads death in any form and wishes to hear as little of it as he can. All that can be added here is that it is a mystical dying that results in raising a man to the Fifth Kingdom and makes him an Initiate and citizen thereof. He suffers a sea change, into something rich and strange. But the change is a subjective one, occurring in his inward parts and transforming his consciousness by a literal renewing of his mind. Other people will see no difference in his outward appearance; he returns to the companions of his former toils and resumes his usual activities, yet his whole being is thenceforth raised to a higher power and reinforced by life of a higher quality and potential.

But of this fifth kingdom Wilmshurst adds one more word, and it is one towards which his previous argument has been leading. This fifth kingdom is a transcendental condition of consciousness that is implied by the eternal flame burning in the Centre of the Lodge. And it comes suddenly, in an eyewink, and we are changed. It is the change, which is experienced, in real Initiation. In that solemn crisis of psychological expansion there comes a rending of one's mental veil, it is subjectively heard ripping and crashing, like the sound of a trumpet as the delicate nerve webbing which had previously shut off perception from super sensual things rips apart and the blinding blaze of light immortal makes you an Initiate.

The Masonic path leads from the fading light of the west and the dark inner thoughts of the dying ego towards the black ignorance of the north. During the dark night of the spirit, we must strive for balance, first within ourselves then without, in our relationship with the cosmos. So next we see the symbol of the fire and the water triangles interlaced about the centre, showing that we have balanced our mind and emotions with our urges and spiritual impulses at which point we can fit this newly balanced individual into the rest of the world. Now the symbol we met in the south appears again. But this time we are not studying it, we are living it. This symbol now shows our personality in balance with the cosmos and our mind has perceived the centre allowing us to reach a new level of consciousness, and the path is now open to the spiritual East.

As the faint light of the bright morning star rises in our spiritual east we meet another symbol of balance and harmony. It is two squares rotated by an angle of 45 degrees. This symbolises the balance of a individual spirit set within a balanced universe. At this point we know our place in the cosmos. The square of our spirit is merged into the square of the cosmos, as represented by the lodge, and we are now in harmony.

Finally we reach the east, and meet the final symbol of the pilgrimage. It is the circle with the centre but now surround by two other triangles. A large upward facing fire triangle containing a smaller downward facing water triangle each centred on the point which is always equidistant from the centre. This is the point from which no Mason can err, the point of universal consciousness where our mind expands to understand our place in the cosmos.

There is one last item on the main part of the tracing board. A ladder reaching from the dark square of the west to the bright, centred triangles of the east. This is the route we can willingly travel from the darkness of the west to the light of the bright morning star raising in our spiritual east.

What then is this centre by which we hope to regain the secrets of our lost nature? We may reason from analogies. As the Divine Will is the centre of the whole universe and controls it; as the sun is the centre and life-giver of our solar system and controls and feeds with life the planets circling round it, so at the secret centre of individual human life exists a vital, immortal principle, the spirit. This is the faculty which, once we have found it, we can never err. It is a point within the circle of our own nature. In this physical world, the circle of our existence is bounded by two grand parallel lines; one representing Moses; the other Solomon, that is to say, law and wisdom; the divine ordinances regulating the universe on the one hand; the divine wisdom and mercy on the other. The Mason who keeps himself thus circumscribed cannot err.

Masonry is a system of philosophy that provides us with a doctrine of the universe and of our place in it. It has three purposes.

Its first purpose is to show that man is but a fragment of a high and holy centre that is isolated at the circumference, or within an ignorant externalized condition; to indicate to those who desire to regain that centre that we can find the centre in ourselves, for, since Deity is as a circle whose centre is everywhere, it follows that a divine centre, a "vital and immortal principle", exists within ourselves.

Its second purpose is to declare the way by which that centre may be found within ourselves, and this teaching is embodied in the discipline and ordeals delineated in the three degrees. The Masonic doctrine of the Centre is in other words that "the Kingdom of Heaven is within you".

Its third purpose is to accept that it is difficult for any individual to discover Truth without the support and guidance of a lodge of willing and dedicated searchers and teachers.

Brethren, may you all come to the knowledge how to open the Lodge upon the centre of yourselves, within the Lodge of your fellow seekers after Truth and so realize in your own conscious experience the finding of the "imprisoned splendour" hidden in the depths of your being, whose rising within you will bring peace and salvation.

Essay 14 - The Influence of Freemasonry on the Life and Work of Bro, Sir Robert Moray, Soldier, Scientist, Spy, Freemason and Founder of the Royal Society.

Freemasonry not only makes good men better but it can also make nasty men into pillars of society.

In the seventeenth century England suffered a devastating Civil War. It began as an argument about the relative importance of the Stuart Kings and their English Parliament, and ended with Charles I having his head cut off. During this turbulent period, magic died and science began.

Somehow, in the midst of the battles between King and Parliament, modern, experimental science popped into being. A country, which burnt alive at least 100 elderly women a year on suspicion that they were causing disease by casting the 'evil eye', spontaneously developed a critical mass of discerning, logical scientists.

To the delight of conspiracy theorists world wide it turns out the whole venture was a politically inspired plot, engineered by a life-long Freemason who shamelessly used his Masonic connections to help out a struggling national administration, which had run out of money.

The secret plan was sprung on the evening of Wednesday 28 Nov, 1660, at Gresham College when an elite society was formed. It became known as the Royal Society, and the dirty deed was done immediately after a Gresham College public lecture given by Christopher Wren. Wren was a confirmed astrologer with an incipient interest in astronomy. (In his inaugural lecture as Professor of Astronomy at Gresham College spoke of how London was particularly favoured by the 'various celestial influences of the different planets, as the seat of the mechanical arts and trade, as well as the liberal sciences'. No modern Professor of Astronomy would make such an astrological claim today.)

The Royal Society is now the oldest and most respected scientific society in the world, its early members' names living on amidst the indexes of physics textbooks. Craftsmen of Physics still learn Hooke's Law, Boyle's Law, Huygen's construction, Newton's Laws, Leibniz's theorem and Brownian motion. And even look with interest at the works of lesser scientists such as Christopher Wren, John Evelyn, John Wilkins, Elias Ashmole, John Flamsteed and Edmund Halley.

But these men were not scientists, they were the last sorcerers. Ashmole belonged to a society of Rosicrucians and was a practicing astrologer; Newton studied and wrote about the Rosicrucian concepts of alchemy; Hooke carried out magical experiments involving spiders and unicorn's horns. But they were all seduced into studying the hidden secrets of nature and science by a man with an unscrupulous political past.

They were an unlikely group of refugees drawn in equal measure from both sides of the Civil War. They were an odd mixture of clergymen and politicians but the eagerly embraced the idea of forbidding the discussion of religion and politics at their meetings. In an age dominated by politics and religion it was a weird thing to do.

But who was behind these machinations? One man, Sir Robert Moray, stands out. He was not much of scientist but he was a first rate fixer and a born survivor. He brought together men with money and men with knowledge, and got them to work together. This essay is a celebration of his achievement.

With the hindsight bred of my scientific education it seems inevitable that the logic of science should succeed in banishing myth and superstition. At the beginning of 1660, however, this outcome was not so certain. Fortunately Moray had a plan at this difficult time to bring together people who turned out to be the important fathers of modern science and he inspired them to develop a new positive logic. I believe it was the positive influence of his initiation into the Lodge of Edinburgh and his study of Masonic concepts which transformed this third-rate chancer into a major benefactor of mankind.

Only five months after Charles II returned to the throne of England Moray brought together a small group of men who kick-started modern science. For scientific method to develop out of a community that believed in magic is an unlikely event. When you add into the mix that almost equal numbers of the founder members of this Royal Society had recently fought on opposite sides of the brutal Civil War, such a fortuitous meeting of minds seems not just improbable, but impossible. How did Moray do it?

If traditional accounts of the formation of the Royal Society are to be believed, the concept of experimental science was developed, and fully formed, independently but simultaneously, on both sides during the Civil War. Then, through a common interest in public lectures, all the members of the two groups happened to meet for tea at Gresham College on a misty November afternoon.

The survivors of a civil war do not seem the most likely people to start a new science club. After the death of Oliver Cromwell the country tottered on the brink of fresh conflict, until the controversial decision was taken to invite the King to return. He had, however, to promise to behave himself. In this chaotic atmosphere of Restoration London the Royal Society began. And it was not cheap to take part. It had an extremely high joining fee and a hefty weekly refresh fee, to be paid whether or not you attended.

During the Civil War sons had been fighting their fathers; brothers trying to kill each other; great estates had been despoiled; a King had been publicly beheaded; and royal princes had fled to exile. For twelve years the country had been run on the personal whim by a military dictator and only the immediate threat of another civil war had persuaded Parliament to restore the King. Yet, like an eye of calm in the midst of these furious storms, we are supposed to accept that these learned men sat calmly chatting about how to develop a radical new philosophy of experimental science. Only the perfect vision of hindsight can make this seem natural.

The founders of the Royal Society questioned the basic premises of religion and theology. Yet they managed to avoid fighting the extreme fanatics who were forcing their views on everybody else. Having successfully avoided the attentions of the Covenanters, the Levellers, the Fifth Monarchists, the Papists and the fanatical followers of the Book of Common Prayer, they seemed free to investigate such heretical matters as the practicality of witchcraft and nobody challenged them.

They seemed to avoid the problems of faith by accepting the Church's view on God and the soul, but questioning everything else. But, if they had been developing such questioning views during the time of Matthew Hopkins, (who as Witch-Finder General in 1647 executed 200 old women for practicing witchcraft) they must have kept quiet about them or they too would have been persecuted. Yet for these ideas to appear twenty three years later fully-formed, suggests they must have been around for a considerable time. By 1660, the members of the Royal Society were giving no credence to witchcraft and were publicly laughing at 'Popish miracles', as proof of superstition.

Why did nobody notice these ideas developing? Why within the first few weeks of the Restoration, did science suddenly break free of the stifling dogma of religious belief and the repressive superstition of magic, and never look back?

The change can be traced directly to the meeting at Gresham College, engineered by Moray and from which grew a society to study the mechanisms of nature. The most inspired move was to forbid the discussion of religion and politics at their meetings. This made sure they were not distracted by dogma. From this group modern experimental science grew.

It seems simple enough. A number of gentlemen met up by accident as they regularly attended the Gresham public lectures in London. They so much enjoyed talking about science that they set up a scientific society to amuse themselves. They weren't short of money so they fixed a ten shilling joining fee and a shilling a week contribution to pay for their amusement (this would equate to about £500 to join and an ongoing fee of £50 per week in today's terms).

But what sort of man was Robert Moray?

Below are three very different aspects Sir Robert Moray.

Sir Robert Moray cannot be taken to be a typical mid-seventeenth century Freemason: the fact that he reveals so much about what Masonry meant to him in itself makes him unique.

DAVID STEVENSON, PROFESSOR OF SCOTTISH HISTORY, UNIVERSITY OF ST ANDREWS

While he [Sir Robert Moray] lived he was the life and soul of that body [The Royal Society]

THE RIGHT REVD. GILBERT BURNETT, BISHOP OF SALISBURY

After he [Cardinal Richelieu] sounded the depth of the man's mind and finding he [Sir Robert Moray] was indifferent, so as he could make a fortune, whether it were with the King or with the malcontented Puritans, he finds no difficulty to persuade him that his love for the Scots, by virtue of their ancient league made him lament their cases.

PATRICK GORDON, SPALDING CLUB, LONDON

Moray is a Freemason who thought deeply about the Craft, recorded in his letters how the teachings of Freemasonry shaped his philosophy and so lets a diligent researcher uncover the influences on his actions.

Moray is an enthusiast and the driving force behind the scientific society he creates.

Moray is a two-timing political chancer whose loyalty can be bought.

These three quotations show different and conflicting aspects of Sir Robert Moray. He is involved in almost every key event that formed the "Society For Promoting Philosophical Knowledge by Experiment". He is the driving force behind turning it into a royal club. The Royal Society was Moray's brainchild; his influence was far more than any other single person.

But Moray was skilled in the dark arts of espionage and concealment. When I first began to study him I did not understand what motivated him He changed sides so often during the Civil Wars it is hard to keep track of him. He was knighted by Charles I, within days of serving as a senior member of the Army that had contributed to the king's downfall and then paid homage to the Royal personage and was knighted. He was ransomed from a Bavarian jail by the French and sent to London to act as their negotiator with the Scots. He persuaded Charles II to be crowned King of Scots, at Scoon, but within a few months was imprisoned for trying to assassinate his new king. He was with Charles II in Paris when General Monck decided to restore the Monarchy, but he did not return to England until three months after the king, and was immediately given a grace and favour home in Whitehall and had prompt access to every philosopher in London. In short he was an enigmatic man.

The only major biography of Moray, published in 1922, does not mention that he was a Freemason. However, the Earl of Elgin has preserved a long series of letters he wrote to Brother Alexander Bruce. This collection is known as the Kincardine Papers and goes into great detail about the importance of Freemasonry to Sir Robert.

During the sixty-five years of his life he worked as a mercenary and spy for the king of France; was Quartermaster general for a Covenanter's Army; almost managed to rescue Charles I from the Scots; was imprisoned and ransomed by the Bavarians; became a negotiator in the arrangements to have Charles II crowned king of Scots at Scoon; led a Scots' rising against Cromwell; was imprisoned for trying to assassinate Charles II; was appointed Privy Counsellor, Lord Justice Clerk and Lord of Session in Edinburgh; worked as a spy for the Earl of Lauderdale; and in his spare time was the life and soul of the Royal Society. And Scottish Freemasonry considers him so important that they created a Lodge of Research named in his honour: Lodge Sir Robert Moray, No 1641.

I decided to take every single fact I could find about him. (He and his actions are mentioned by most of the great diarists of the period,) I took all these facts, arranged them in date order and used the historical context of the times to illuminate his actions. Using modern techniques of data collection and collation I set out to see him clearly and to try to understand him. What emerged from this mass of inchoate facts was the picture of an intelligent and ambitious man who was inspired and transformed by exposure to the philosophy of Freemasonry. Not a good man made better by the Craft but a rather nasty man made into a good man by putting into practice the Masonic ideals he learned.

So let's look at his achievement. Who were the men who Moray brought together to found the Royal Society?

Well their most important common factor is that they were all regular attendees at Gresham public lectures. So I'll begin by looking at each in turn starting with the man who took the chair at the first meeting of the Royal Society, John Wilkins.

The Right Revd John Wilkins – Parliamentarian

Wilkins was born in 1614 at Fawsley in Northamptonshire. He was the son of an Oxford goldsmith and the grandson of country vicar, John Dodd. He went on to be a successful churchman himself. By the time he died, in 1672, he was bishop of Chester.

During the Civil War, Wilkins was a great supporter of Parliament and he got his reward. On 12 April 1648, (after Charles I's surrender to the Scots at Newark), he was made Warden of Wadham College, Oxford. The job was vacant because Parliament threw out the previous warden, for holding Royalist sympathies. Eleven years later Wilkins successfully sought a special ruling from the Lord Protector, Oliver Cromwell, that he might 'be relieved of the prohibition against marriage' that was a requirement of his post. As soon as this was granted he married Cromwell's sister Robina.

Whatever Wilkin's motive for getting wed, the match helped his career. One of Cromwell's last acts before dying was to order Parliament to appoint him Master of Trinity College, Cambridge. This was confirmed by Robina's nephew Richard Cromwell, who briefly became the Protector after his father's death.

Wilkins plan for rapid preferment fell apart, however, when Charles II returned to the throne. He was deposed as Master of Trinity College and the once favoured brother- in-law to Cromwell was reduced to preaching for coppers. He was struggling to live, crammed into the squalid lodging of yet another deposed cleric and reduced to acting as a chaplain for the penny pinching lawyers of Gray's Inn. Wilkins presented such a sorry spectacle that he was beginning to attract voyeurs to the Temple church, just to marvel at the extent to which the family of the late Lord Protector could be humiliated.

So when Wilkins chaired that fateful meeting on Wednesday 28 November, 1660, he was in dire circumstances. He was an object of curiosity for the more literate men of London; he had lost his Mastership; he was homeless; and he had been driven from his new job in Cambridge. Reduced to sharing the lodgings of Seth Ward, Wilkins must have been hard pressed to find the substantial subscription needed to join the new Society.

Viscount William Brouncker – Royalist

Brouncker was a Royalist who had kept his head down during Cromwell's rule. He spent his time translating Descartes theories about music into English. He was also a capable mathematician. Brouncker had studied under John Wallis, the Savilian professor of Geometry at Oxford, who was a friend of John Wilkins. As a signatory of the Declaration of 1660, Brouncker had played his part in the Restoration when he was returned as MP for Westbury in the Convention Parliament.

Brouncker wanted to be sure that the newly restored King knew of his loyalty, so he made Charles a gift of a small pleasure craft, which he named The Greyhound. He had designed it on radical new lines, and gave the King this gift 'to mark his restoration to the throne of England'. He was on the opposite side of the political fence to John Willkins and his fortunes were moving in the opposite direction. Brouncker had just recovered political power while Wilkins was a discredited down and out.

The Right Honourable Robert Boyle - Parliamentarian

Robert Boyle was thirty-three years old and had spent most of the Civil War writing theological tracts in the depths of Dorset. During the early part of the Protectorate he moved to Ireland but in 1653 John Wilkins, wrote to him inviting him to Wadham College, to continue his studies of nature and science. Boyle moved to Oxford in 1654. He proved an extremely competent physicist and gave his name to the law that relates the pressure and the volume of a gas. He stayed in Oxford until 1668 when he moved to London. If he was a regular attendee at the Wednesday afternoon lectures at Gresham College he must also have been a regular traveller. Gresham College, then in Bishopsgate Street, was a 120 mile round trip from his home, near the Three Tuns public house in Oxford. With more than a day's ride each way he would have had little time left for anything else, so it seems safe to assume Robert Boyle did not make it his usual custom to attend the lectures on Wednesday afternoons. But he did sometimes come up to London to stay with his sister in Chelsea, as John Evelyn visited him there on 7 September 1660. However, the lecture to be given by Christopher Wren must have attracted him enough to make the journey and somebody may have encouraged him to come. Who might that have been? As his ex-tutor, perhaps it was John Wilkins.

Alexander Bruce, Second Earl of Kincardine - Royalist

Bruce was a Scotsman and the younger brother of Edward, the first Earl of Kincardine. Edward Bruce had been made an earl by Charles I in 1647. The Bruce family supported the Stuarts throughout the Civil War. After Charles II's abortive attempt to drive out Cromwell, in 1650, Alexander was forced to flee to exile in Breman. He remained there until 1660, when he went to The Hague to join Charles II for his return to London. He travelled back to London with Charles's entourage and set up house in Charing Cross.

Bruce's health was poor after his return from exile and he stayed in London recuperating until 1662. That year he succeeded to his brother's title and returned to live in Culross, Scotland. A series of Wednesday afternoon lectures on science sounds just the sort of thing to cheer him up, during his convalescence, so he might have been 'regular attendee', at least after the Restoration. Or was he invited by his long-time personal friend Sir Robert Moray?

Dr Jonathan Goddard - Parliamentarian

Goddard was a medical man, who had obtained his doctorate of medicine from Cambridge in 1643, at the age of 26. He was been appointed Professor of Physic at Gresham College in 1655, but had been Warden of Merton College, Oxford. Goddard had the best of both worlds. Perhaps he was allowed such license because he was Oliver Cromwell's personal physician. He held his Gresham appointment in absentia and continued to live in Oxford, and to draw the warden's stipend, until Charles II summarily dismissed him. Goddard was friendly with Wilkins while he was at Oxford. But when Charles purged Oxford of Parliamentarians, Goddard decided it was time to fall back on his Gresham professorship, and he moved back to live in his College rooms. Many of the early Society meetings were held in his rooms at Gresham. The college was important when the Royal Society was being formed and I couldn't help wondering why so many Gresham professors came to support a 'Royal' Society so soon after being thrown out of better paying university posts by the newly restored King.

Sir Paul Neile - Royalist

Neile was born in 1613 and had been a courtier to Charles I. For his service as an usher of the Privy Chamber he had been knighted in 1633. In 1640 he was elected MP for Ripon during the Short Parliament but during Cromwell's rule Neile wisely lived quietly near Maidenhead, keeping a low profile. He remains almost invisible until the minute books of the Royal Society start to report some of his activities. It is clear that he was very much an amateur scientist whose particular skill was the grinding of optical glasses for use in telescopes. It was this private interest in the production of high quality optics which first brought together the, then disgraced, courtier and the powerful Warden of Wadham College. Indeed Neile had such skill at grinding lenses that John Wilkins preferred to spend his honeymoon with Sir Paul, talking about the grinding process, rather than with his new bride. Perhaps this was a wise move, considering the advanced age of Robina Cromwell (she was a widow of sixty-two years of age at the time of her marriage).

Dr William Petty - Parliamentarian

Petty invented the craft of statistics. He developed techniques of recording and analysing the detail of political events involving large numbers of people, and laid the basis for the modern Office of Government Statistics. Born in 1623 he served as ship's boy before joining the Royal Navy. He retained an interest in ships and shipping for the rest of his life. When the Civil War broke out, Petty left England. He went to Paris to study medicine and chemistry and while he was there he met Thomas Hobbes and Decartes. He returned to London, after the defeat of the King, and was well placed when Parliament removed many of the incumbents of high office at the Universities and replaced them with its own supporters. He became a fellow of Brasenose College, Oxford and was awarded an MD. By 1650 he occupied the Chair of Anatomy at Brasenose and was also created the Professor of Music at Gresham College. His real success, however came when he took two year's leave of absence from his academic positions to go to Ireland as chief physician to Cromwell's army. There he earned a good reputation as a military medic. Once Cromwell's army had subdued Ireland the seized lands had to be redistributed and new titles of ownership created. In December 1654 he offered to complete a new survey of the whole of Ireland within thirteen months. He succeeded brilliantly and his 'Down Survey' still forms the basis of the legal record of title for a large proportion of the land holdings of Ireland.

During his time in Ireland Petty met Robert Boyle, who became his patient and friend. Through Petty, Boyle met the 'Parliamentary High Table Group' (including Wilkins). These were academics who had replaced Royalists and now held all the senior positions at Oxford. Petty became independently wealthy from his successful survey of Ireland. However, he still held his Oxford and Gresham College appointments 'in absentia' and drew both stipends. In the late fifties Petty began to take a practical interest in the design of efficient sailing vessels. He started to work on designs for double hulled (catamaran type vessels) which had the potential to greatly outpace contemporary ships.

He had been such a strong supporter of Parliament, during the period of the commonwealth, that in late 1660 he was stripped of the Vice-presidency of Brasenose College, Oxford. He went to live in Gresham, keeping his head down with the other refugees. The Chair of Music at Gresham College was the only academic post he managed to hold onto. Perhaps it is hardly surprising that he met up with his old colleagues, who had also been ousted from their cosy University posts by the newly returned King. As he was in residence at Gresham College his attendance at Wren's lecture on 28 Nov 1660 did not surprise me, but why he wanted to help found a Royal Society was a puzzle. He had no reason to like the King or hope for the monarch's patronage.

Mr William Ball - Royalist

Ball, was an amateur scientist and a Royalist. Charles II chose him to be the Royal Society's first treasurer. Prior to the 28 Nov meeting Ball had been co-operating with John Wallis to study the rings of the planet Saturn. Between 1656 and 1659 Wallis wrote a series of letters to the Dutch astronomer and mathematician, Christiaan Huygens. In these letters he reported the results of Ball's observations. Huygens went on to quote Ball's work in his own theory of the nature of Saturn and its satellites. Huygens visited Ball's London home on 1 May 1661. On the evening of that visit Mr Ball held a dinner to celebrate the first anniversary of Parliament's reading of Charles II's Declaration of Breda. The acceptance of this statement by Parliament paved the way for the King's return from The Hague in May 1660. Sir Robert Moray, who had spent some years in the Nederlands, was also invited.

Mr Laurence Rooke - Parliamentarian

Laurence Rooke was the host of the meeting of 28 November. At the time he was Professor of Geometry at Gresham College and aged thirty-eight years. He had gained his degree from King's College Cambridge in 1643 and then retired for three years to live in the country. He seems never to have enjoyed good health. Indeed, he was not even fit enough to graduate. His degree was awarded 'in absentia' as he was not strong enough to attend the ceremony. He went to live in Kent after completing his degree. This retirement to the country seemed to strengthen him and in 1650 he moved to Wadham College, to study under John Wilkins and Seth Ward. He also met, and worked, with Robert Boyle. The fact he was acceptable at Oxford confirms he was a Parliamentary supporter, as all Royalists were ousted from the universities. After two years working at Oxford he was offered the Professorship of Astronomy at Gresham College, a post he held for five years until he became the Gresham Professor of Geometry in 1657.

Rooke's main area of interest was the measurement of longitude. His first ideas were to use sightings of the moon or the movements of the moons of Jupiter. He wrote papers on methods for observing lunar eclipses for 'the geographical purpose of determining terrestrial longitude'. Rooke knew that the movement of shadows on the moon's surface can be used as an accurate clock. The jagged peaks of the mountains of the moon act like the pointer on a sundial and he thought that the various craters and rifts could make up the scale of this celestial clock. As the moon was visible from everywhere on the earth's surface the moment of shadow contact happened at the same time for every watcher. Rooke recognized the moon as a giant sundial hanging high in full view of the whole world. All that was needed to know your longitude was to measure the altitude of a first magnitude star and compare it with its altitude at the same time for the home port.

Charles II was so impressed with the idea that he asked for a demonstration showing this effect. His instructions, sent via Sir Robert Moray, asked for a large scale globe model of the moon to be constructed 'representing not only the spots and various degrees of whiteness upon the surface, but the hills, eminences and cavities moulded in solid work.' The model was built by Christopher Wren and presented to the King's private museum. It was set up on a rotating stand so that it could be illuminated and turned to reveal all the phases of the moon 'with the variety of appearances that happen from the shadows of the mountains and valleys.'

The idea is ingenious and works well, if the sky is clear enough to allow a detailed view of the moon and the mariner is a skilled astronomer, familiar with the surface features of the moon. In addition, the sailor would need an ephemeris showing the positions of the main stars.

Rooke was an intensely practical man, capable of original thought. His practicality, however, did not extend to taking care of his own health. He caught a chill, while walking home without his coat, after a visit to the house of his patron the Marquis of Dorchester, and died on 26 June 1662.

Sir Christopher Wren - Parliamentarian

Christopher Wren was born on 20 October 1632 in a little village about sixteen miles from Salisbury. His mother died when he was only two years old and the following year his father, also called Christopher, was appointed Dean of Windsor and Registrar of the Order of the Garter. The earliest memories of young Christopher would have been those of living in the grounds of Windsor Castle and mixing with its Royal occupants. The Installation of Charles II, a boy only slightly older than himself as the Prince of Wales and a Knight of the Garter must have impressed him. As Dean of Windsor, his father took part in the ceremony on 12 May 1638.

Prince Charles Louis, the exiled Elector Palatine was also

staying at the Deanery of Windsor. The Elector had as his personal chaplain a young clergyman who has already figured in this story, John Wilkins. At this stage of Wren's life both he and the Revd Wilkins were clearly in the Royalist camp.

Something happened, in 1642 that decided Wilkins that he would fare better on the side of Parliament whilst young Christopher was celebrating his tenth birthday. A troop of Roundhead soldiers, led by a Captain Fogg, seized the Deanery of Windsor and ransacked it. The Wren family fled first to Bristol and then to Bicester, near Oxford. (Wilkins fled to London. He did not side with the Royalists again until after the 28 November meeting and the Restoration forced his hand.)

Christopher Wren senior remained a firm supporter of the King. First, at Bristol, and then, after Bristol had fallen to Lord Fairfax, in Oxford. (Charles had moved his Parliament to Oxford at that time.) In an attempt to keep his son out of the hostilities Wren senior sent Christopher to school in London, where he met up with John Wilkins, now a supporter of Parliament and Warden of Wadham College, Oxford. In 1650, aged eighteen years, Christopher went up to Wadham College to study. Wilkins became Wren's protector, something he certainly needed in those difficult times as his father had faced serious charges from Roundhead purists. They said that the decorative plaster work he had created in his Church at East Knoyle, was too ornate and papist! Wren senior was severely censured and lost his living while Wren junior prospered at Oxford, under the patronage of Wilkins.

In 1657 Christopher Wren was appointed to the Gresham Chair of Astronomy. To mark his preferment Sir Paul Neile, an old friend of the Wren family from their days in Windsor, gave Christopher a new telescope. Wren used it to good effect during the four years he stayed at Gresham. Wren left Gresham, in 1661, to take up the job of Savilian Professor of Astronomy at Oxford. This was the post Seth Ward had been ejected from by Charles II only twelve months earlier.

Mr Abraham Hill - Uncommitted

Hill seems a very odd choice for a founder of the Royal Society. His main virtue was that he was rich. He was only twenty-five years old but early in 1660 both his parents died leaving him a moderate fortune. He had no need to work to keep himself and as he had not benefited from a University education he decided to take advantage the public lectures offered by Gresham College.

He was a regular listener to Gresham lectures and so perhaps it was natural for him to be invited to the discussions afterwards. He was certainly keen on the early experimental proceedings of the new Society, serving on many committees and assisting the more learned members with various experiments

Sir Robert Moray - Covenanter/French Spy/Royalist

Sir Robert Moray was also a Scot. He was born 10 March 1609 and educated at St Andrews University before serving with the Scots Guards of Louis XIII in 1633. Towards the end of Cardinal Richelieu's life Moray became his favourite and then acted as a spy for him. In 1638 the General Assembly of the Covenanters in Scotland were rebelling against Charles I. Richelieu gave Moray a commission, promoting him to Lieutenant-Colonel in Louis's elite Scots Guards, and dispatched him to Scotland. Ostensibly he was supposed to recruit more Scots soldiers but he also admitted that he had the objective of assisting his fellow countrymen in their dispute with Charles, by causing trouble for England.

Moray was appointed quartermaster-general of the Covenanter's Army, in 1640. He was responsible for laying out camps and fortifications, where his knowledge of mathematics and surveying would have been extremely important. He marched south with the Scottish Army towards the Tyne and played his part in defeating the Earl Stafford's English conscript Army at Newcastle. On 20 May 1641 Moray was initiated in to Freemasonry whilst garrisoned at Newcastle the Masonic officers who initiated him were General Alexander Hamilton, commander of the Coventantor' Army in Newcastle and John Mylne, Master Mason to King Charles I.

By 1643 he was acting as a liaison officer between the Covenanters' Army and Charles I, in his court at Oxford. On 10 Jan 1643, Charles knighted him. Soon afterward Sir Robert returned to France and was promoted to full Colonel in the Scots Guards. He was captured by the Duke of Barvaria while leading his regiment into battle on the 24 Nov 1643 and was imprisoned for eighteen months. He was freed on 28 April 1645 when the French decided to pay a ransom of £16,500 for him.

After the execution of Charles I, and at the request of the Earl of Lauderdale, Moray opened negotiations that led to Charles II going to Scotland to be crowned King of Scots at Scoon in 1650. Charles's campaign, with a Scots army, to recover England from Cromwell failed at the Battle of Dunbar and, after hiding for a while in an oak tree, Charles fled to France. Moray stayed in Scotland.

Soon after Charles's flight Moray married Sophia Lindsey, the sister of the Earl of Balcarres. In July 1652 the newly married Morays returned to Edinburgh for the birth of their first child, and also to help organize a rising to restore Charles to the throne of England, but neither was to be. Sophia suffered a protracted and agonizing labour before finally dying, on 2 Jan 1653, with the still born child.

The Scots were defeated by Cromwell at the battle of Loch Garry in July 1654. Moray was accused of betraying the King but was cleared after writing directly to him and appealing his innocence. Moray returned to France, he never remarried.

By 1655 Moray was back in Paris. At 46 he was getting too old for the Scots Guards. He resigned his commission and after spending a year in Bruges went to Maastricht where he spent his time studying science and carrying out that protracted correspondence with Alexander Bruce. In September 1659 he went to Paris to meet with Charles and proceeded to take part in the negotiations with General Monck to have Charles restored to throne of England.

When the King returned to England, in late June 1660, Moray stayed on in Paris for some months. When he traveled to London, in August, contemporaries reported the King greeted him warmly. 'His Majesty received Robert Moray with crushing and shaking of his hand.' Charles immediately found him a grace and favour house within the grounds of the Palace of Whitehall. A drawing of Whitehall in 1680, held by the London Topographical Society, shows Sir Robert's quarters to be a small house situated just inside the Horse Guards Gate and looking out over the privy garden. The site of this house was exactly opposite where Dover House now stands on the present Whitehall.

It was from this house that Sir Robert set out to Gresham College on 28th November. He had been living in London for three months, having spent the previous ten years in exile. He could hardly have been a regular attendee of the Gresham meetings during this time. By now I was very interested to try to discover why he decided to attend Gresham College for Wren's lecture. But I also wondered just how did a French spy come to know Oliver Cromwell's brother in law? Let alone be invited to a meeting with so many disgruntled Parliamentarians, who so history tells us, unanimously elected Cromwell's brother in law to chair them.

The original founders of the Royal Society split into two major groupings. About half were Royalists who had kept out of public life during the rule of Cromwell and returned to London to seek advancement at the court of King Charles II; whilst the other half were Parliamentarian academics who had taken control of the Universities under Cromwell but had been thrown out of virtually everywhere, except Gresham College, when Charles had returned. Add into this mix one independently wealthy young man who was following a voluntary course in self education, again at Gresham, and you have a pretty clear picture of the founders. Now let's look at the role of Robert Moray in bringing them together.

By plotting the movements of the king and individuals named about it emerged that only one of these original founders had any real influence with the King. That was Sir Robert Moray. But this ex-French spy and monarchist rabble-rouser is out of place among the Parliamentary Puritans of the Gresham set. His only link to them is via Freemasonry.

On 5 December 1660 the minutes of the Society show that:

'Sir Robert Moray brought in word from the Court, that the King had been acquainted with the designe of the Meeting. And he did well approve of it, and would give encouragement to it.'

This was only a week after the very first meeting. So Sir Robert was either extremely eager to please his new Puritan friends, or he had already prepared his ground.

As a boy, Robert Moray was fascinated by civil engineering and inspired by the undersea mine which George Bruce built under the Firth of Forth. After studying at St Andrew's University he became a soldier and then a politician. While serving in the Army he became a Freemason, and found that the ideas and philosophy of Freemasonry complemented his love of science and met his need for spiritual fulfilment which had not been satisfied by conventional religion. Freemasonry encouraged his innate love of symbolism and helped him think things through for himself to develop distinct ideas throughout his life. His self-sufficiency often provoked his enemies but he had learned from Freemasonry to be cautious in his responses. He once wrote of himself: 'I have been reported to be writing against Scripture, an Atheist, a Magician or Necromancer, and a malignant for ought I know by half a Kingdom.' It did not seem to bother him greatly. Nor did it seem to worry Charles II. The King was as cynical as Sir Robert. Charles II has been described as a King indifferent to religion who let Moray go his own way, remarking teasingly that he believed Moray to be head of his own church.

But accommodation with the Stuart Kings came later in Robert's life. As a young soldier he showed a talent for manipulation and espionage, and a weakness for the glamour of the French Court, which worked against Charles I.

As an agent for the French he was active in the events leading up to the impeachment of Charles. Moray used his membership of the Lodge of Edinburgh, which had among its members many of the Scottish courtiers of Charles I and General Hamilton (who had initiated into Freemasonry Moray at Newcastle), to improve his network of contacts. The Stuarts and their court had been involved with Freemasonry since 1601, when James VI(I) had been initiated into Freemasonry at Scoon as part of William Schaw's plan to establish Royal patronage for Freemasonry.

Moray was adopted by Cardinal Richelieu to spy against the English. He seems to have carried out this role with great relish for as long as Richelieu supported him. Moray carried the news of Richelieu's death to Charles I at Oxford. Moray's connections with the Freemasons of Charles's Scottish Court may have persuaded the King that he could be trusted as in 1642 Charles knighted Sir Robert to give him sufficient status to act as the British King's messenger to the King of France.

When Moray returned to France and delivered Charles's message he was promoted for his efforts. Then he went on active service in Bavaria where he was unlucky enough to be captured and imprisoned. Louis XIII died and Cardinal Mazarin seized power over France. The new King, Louis XIV was too young to rule. Mazarin was not interested in Moray and left him to languish in prison. He was only ransomed when Mazarin saw a chance to use him in the bargaining between Charles and his English Parliament. Moray's Masonic connections with the leading

Covenanters were the key to his importance. Moray was sent to London where General Hamilton was leading the Scots delegation. Mazarin only bought Moray out of prison to use his Masonic connections and work as an *agent provocateur* against Charles.

Sir Robert came close to persuading Charles I to flee to France, where he would have become a useful pawn for Mazarin. But Charles lost his nerve, after Moray dressed him up as a woman to try to get him passed the guards. Moray could have so compromised the Stuart line, by persuading Charles I to seek exile in France, that Cromwell would have created an enduring English Republic. However, Charles did not get to France, he was subsequently put on trial, found guilty of treason and executed.

After the death of Charles I, Moray left the French Army and returned to Edinburgh. He renewed his contacts with his Edinburgh Lodge, its minutes record his attendance at meetings. He married Sophia Lindsey and started to become less mercenary. Up to that time his talents had been for sale and France paid him well. But after his short, tragic marriage (Sophia died in child birth less than a year after the marriage) and his subsequent retreat into contemplation of Masonic symbolism and philosophy he became much more loyal.

He got to know Charles II at a time when the young man was under tremendous religious and political pressure from the Presbyterians and warmed to him. From then on he seems to have used all his undoubted military and political skills to support the new Stuart King of Scots.

He assisted in the negotiations for Charles II's Coronation, at Scoon. After the death of his wife, Moray became closer to Charles II and organized an uprising on his behalf in the Highlands. When Lord Glencairn falsely accused Moray of plotting against the young King, Moray made a peculiar Masonic appeal to Charles to protest his innocence. After receiving this letter Charles spoke up in his defense. Moray's choice of words when appealing to the King drew attention to his ongoing involvement with Freemasonry.

He wrote 'Your Majesty may, do with me as a Master Builder doth with his material':

Later Moray worked for Charles, against the Roundheads, in the Highlands and he remained loyal even after being imprisoned and falsely accused of plotting to kill the King. Once his name had been cleared Moray used his influence in France to help the King's cause. Charles had fled to France, to join his mother, after the Roundhead invasion of Scotland. Moray later became part of Charles' court in Paris and then moved with the King to Bruges.

After the death of Cromwell it looked likely that Charles II would be restored to the throne of England. Charles was close to his sister, who was married to the Duke of Orange and from her he knew that the naval war with the Dutch, that Cromwell had started, was likely to flare up again. Moray was either asked, or volunteered, to use his Masonic contacts to gain as much military information about intentions of the Dutch states as he could. He went to Maastricht, where he collected political and military information about the intentions of the Nederlanders. His correspondence shows he used his Freemasonic links to join the local Masons and on the basis of this acceptance became a citizen of Maastricht. I believe that the purpose of Moray's spying missions was to size up the Dutch threat and then return to Paris to assess the likely French response before finally joining the King in London.

Once Charles was settled back in Whitehall, Moray joined him. When he arrived in London he was greeted as an old friend, 'the King gripping and shaking his hand', like a brother and was given private apartments in the Palace of Whitehall with regular access to the King. Moray, brought back the worrying news that the Dutch navy outclassed Charles's fleet and that a resumption of the naval war was extremely likely. Charles had no money and little expertise to call on to improve his navy. He had a great enthusiasm for naval matters but no resources. What could be done, without any naval experts, or the money hire them?

Moray came up with an inspired solution. He exploited his Masonic contacts in and around London, probably using Bro. Bruce to find out just who was involved in studying 'the hidden mysteries of nature and science', the subject that eventually became the centrepiece of the Masonic Second Degree. Within weeks Moray had made contact with Masonic groups which were supporting the 'poor and distressed' brethren who had been thrown out of academic office by the return of a Royalist Government.

He quickly discovered that the main centre for Freemasonry, in Restoration London, was Gresham College. Gresham was a public college which Sir Thomas Gresham had set up to support what Moray saw as the Masonic ideals of study. Here Moray found the answer to Charles's dilemma. When the King had returned to England he had thrown many of the Parliamentarian scientists out of their University posts in an almost knee-jerk response, they were struggling to survive. An important group was based at Gresham College, surviving on the small stipends the College paid to either them or their friends. They represented a pool of expertise in naval technology that could be tapped into. But these 'scientists' were all politically out of favour as well as extremely short of money. And Charles could not afford to pay them.

Moray, however, was resourceful. He had many contacts with the Masonic Scottish nobles and knew many wealthy gentlemen Masons. These Freemasons were not only amateurs, interested in the study of science, but they had money and influence. Moray saw a way of harnessing these two groups and persuading them to work together for the good of their King and country. He saw that he could use his Masonic contacts to solve the problems of Charles's navy.

Moray brought together Royalists with money and Parliamentarians with scientific skills, to set up a self-funding group to solve the pressing problems of sorting out the Navy. Moray, the soldier, was afraid of another war with the Dutch and he realised that their ship-building skills were far in advance of the

English ones at the time. His solution touched the imagination of the newly restored Kingdom. He used the interest in studying the hidden mysteries of nature and science, which was shared by all Freemasons, as a basis for a new Society to focus the application of science on the problems of defense.

Sir Robert encouraged his friends and contacts to attend the weekly lecture, held by one of the bright stars of the Parliamentary scientists, Christopher Wren. It would seem that only two of these founders had no links to Freemasonry. These were Christopher Wren and Robert Boyle. They are recorded as being at the first meeting but have also been added to the list of members drawn up at the meeting to be the first to be invited to join. This omission can be explained if they had left before Moray and his Brother Masons got down to the detailed discussion of setting up a new society to study the Masonic objective of the hidden mysteries of nature and science. Although William Preston asserts that Wren became a Freemason at a later date, Robert Boyle never joined the Craft as he would not take an oath under any circumstances.

To make his idea work Moray took from Freemasonry the injunction not to speak about religion or politics within the meetings. And he drew funds by appealing to the charity of those who could afford it, so enabling able, but poor, men to be able to carry out experiments.

Moray won the confidence of the Parliamentary Masons when he made sure that their deposed leader, John Wilkins, took the chair of that first meeting. Wilkins had been extremely close to Cromwell and his family. By rehabilitating him with the King, Moray showed the other Parliamentary scientists that they were all equal in the new Masonically inspired scientific body he was creating. He laid his ground carefully and, despite the King's busy schedule, Moray reported back to the group, within a week, that they would receive a Royal Charter.

For the first two years he drove and chivvied the group towards his vision of a new scientific Navy. He was satirized as this verse about him shows:

> The Prime Virtuoso hath undertaken
> Through all the Experiments to run
> Of that learned man, Sir Francis Bacon
> Shewing which can, which can't be done.

Moray made sure that most of the scientists, among these first members, had an interest in subjects that mattered to the Navy. He encouraged ship designers, navigation experts and weapons specialists to contribute to the early work. At first he made sure that he chaired the majority of the meetings, to establish a structured form of meeting. He followed an agenda and kept minutes; ways of working he had learned from the Schaw Masonic Lodges of Scotland. The two basic rules he laid down were; all men were welcome to join, irrespective of politics, race or religion; and during meetings only scientific matters were to be discussed, religion and politics being expressly forbidden.

Moray succeeded in creating something far greater than he had ever dreamed of. As the Society developed, it took on a life of its own and soon separated from its Masonic roots. Moray groomed others to take over the day to day tasks of running the meetings and devoted himself to drawing up a charter for his brain child. As the society grew it took in many others who were not Masons.

When the First Charter was delivered Moray stood back, putting forward the Naval enthusiast, Lord Bouncker as the First President, hoping that the Society would now continue under its own momentum. Perhaps he hoped to spend more time working on the History of Freemasonry which he had started to write and encouraging the free exchange of information through his proposed 'Transactions'. He was successful in establishing The Transactions, but his History of Freemasonry was lost when the Hanoverian Duke of Sussex 're-organised' the Royal Society's library at the beginning of the nineteenth century and purged it of any Stuart history.

The first sign that Moray's society was developing into something more than a specialized Masonic Committee to support the King, came when he presented the First Charter to his Royal Society. The fellows did not like the title, which perhaps was too much of an indication of Moray's intent. They wanted a title that linked them with science, not just with Royalty. Its members insisted on a title which made them more than just a 'Society for Supporting the King', they became a Society for the pursuit of knowledge, which was patronized by the King. However, the principle Moray had established of mixing together wealthy amateurs to provide the funds and less wealthy scientists, to do the work of experimentation proved to be sound for the next two hundred years.

Moray's Masonic philosophy was inherited by the new Society and it led to the nurturing of the most important scientific developments of all time. The problems faced by Charles' navy were the problems of understanding the Universe. By developing techniques to aid navigation the founders of the Royal Society created techniques and technology which enabled their members to study the stars. The policy of carrying out flamboyant demonstrations spread the ideas of science to the more influential layers of society. By using the microscope to investigate minute creature to amuse the nobility the science of biology was discovered. Finally the policy of publishing the results of studies and experiments increased the rate of innovation. In less than twenty years the study of the stars had moved from the lore of astrology to the practical application of Newton's Laws to predict the return of Halley's Comet. It is a whimsical thought that the first edition of Old Moore's Almanac was published just seven years before Newton's study of the heavens turned Francis Moore's science of Astrology into mere superstition.

The newly formed Royal Society was a potent package which took a lively group of thinkers and gave them funding; encouragement; and a means of sharing knowledge. Without the change in attitude to the study of the skies which the Royal Society had achieved Newton might never have been published. Less than a generation earlier, while Bacon was writing of his Solomon's House, Galileo was persecuted by the Church for daring to suggest the Earth might revolve around the sun!

All Freemasons today recite the formal statement of the Galileon heresy which forms part of the test questions of the Fellowcraft Degree. I like to think of this as a permanent memorial to the work of Bro Sir Robert Moray in putting into practice his Masonic Oath to 'study the hidden secrets of Nature and Science in Order to better know his Maker'.

I find it hard to believe that Sir Robert set out to create the world's premier Scientific Society on 28 Nov 1660. He probably only expected the group to solve the military problems Charles could not afford to tackle. However, he used the Masonic principles which he learned after his Initiation into the Lodge of Edinburgh. Powerful Masonic ideas of equality and the virtue of observing nature to understand the plan of the Great Architect, which Moray introduced, spawned a tremendous living force. His group was free from the shackles of religious dogma and had a unique democratic structure for its time. Whether by accident, or design, he used four of the most powerful ideas of Freemasonry and applied them to the development of technology.

These were the ideas he took from Freemasonry.

1. That the study of the works of nature can lead to an understanding of the underlying plan of God. i.e. that there is an underlying order of the laws of nature that can be determined by observation and experiment. This idea led directly to the work of Newton.

2. That all men are equal. If they come together to discuss learning, and forbid discussion of religion and politics they will be able to co-operate. This concentration on experimental science to the exclusion of all distractions helped the Royal Society become a major force in creating

our modern scientific age.

3. That for Officers and Presidents to have true power, they must be elected by and have the support of the members they rule. William Schaw, the First Grand Warden of Freemasonry, had decreed that way of working sixty years earlier, and Moray built the idea into the Charters of the Society, ensuring that the Fellows would elect their own leaders so that they would be loyal to them.

4. That wealthy Masons should assist their poor and distressed brethren and give them work. Moray implemented this principle by bringing wealthy amateurs into the Society to fund less wealthy scientists. He encouraged scientists, who had been strong supporters of Parliament and were now suffering great distress, to sit down and meet with wealthy Royalists, who in turn helped fund their work and assist their rehabilitation into Restoration society.

These principles proved to be a sound foundation for building a scientific institution. But, ironically, these Masonic principles only lasted until the Presidency of another Freemason, the Duke of Sussex. Inspired by his own political motives, Sussex "reformed" the library of the Royal Society and in the process "lost" Sir Robert Moray's *History of Masonry*. Sussex was worried about the strong links between the deposed Stuart line and Freemasonry, which had been controlled in the Craft by the forced merger of the Antients and Moderns into the United Grand Lodge, under his Grand Mastership. The Royal Society was the only other place where evidence of the politically dangerous Jacobite roots of Freemasonry might survive. Sussex succeeded in neutralizing the risk and in doing so completely de-Masonified the Royal Society. Now the society limits its members to scientists of world wide renown, without any wealthy amateurs. But fortunately it maintains Moray's first three Masonic principles.

This is my explanation of the unlikely success of the Royal Society. It was founded by an astute, politically motivated, ambitious and untrustworthy Freebooter, who was changed by exposure to Freemasonry into a better man. He never completely rose above his political motivation, but by practicing Masonic ideals he became the Father of Modern Science and a great benefactor of mankind.

His motive was to solve a short term crisis in military technology for a run down Navy. But Sir Robert Moray stole the structure and philosophy of Freemasonry and used it to build a totally new type of organization. The ideas he used were so subversive and powerful that they soon outgrew Moray's limited aims and his Royal Society drew up for itself a much wider agenda, taking the best of Moray's ideas and applying them to its own choice of problems.

Its new attitudes to knowledge and the study of the hidden mysteries of nature and science led to the successful study of physics and the theories of Newton. Natural Philosophy became a predictive science and superstition flowered into technology.

We owe our modern society, and its many wonderful scientific gadgets, to the accidental success of Bro. Sir Robert Moray. He was inspired and improved by the wisdom of the Masonic teachings, which had inspired him; he used methods tried and test with the Scottish Schaw Lodge system to promote harmony and bring together the opposing sides after the great civil war; and he provided a structure that enabled science to break free of the superstitious cage of religion.

No matter how carefully anyone analyzes a complex situation they will not be able to foresee all the possible outcomes of their actions. This is certainly true of the founder of the Royal Society. Moray, reformed-mercenary, talented-spy and master manipulator, probably only expected to solve some of the problems of naval technology and he motivated his opponents by bribing them with a route of preferment and a chance to win back some of their lost position in society. But this small lodge of individuals achieved more than any of them could have done individually. They created a system that brought about a vast increase in human well-being, more than any other in recorded history.

Scientific method started with the work of the Royal Society and it in turn was inspired by Moray's understanding of the inspirational teachings of Freemasonry. Later political events may well have made it expedient for the Hanoverian Monarchy to forget the debt our society has to Scottish Jacobite Freemasonry and the United Grand Lodge of England may prefer to be coy about its Scottish roots but hasn't enough time now passed for the threat of a Jacobite revival which inspired this attitude to be discounted?

Surely now Freemasons can freely celebrate the story of how our Craft gave birth to modern Science and honour the memory of reformed reprobate Bro. Sir Robert Moray, spy, soldier and scientist who conceived the Royal Society, nurtured it through nine months of early presidencies and finally gave it birth through its founding Charters.

Reference: The Invisible College. - The Secret History of How the Freemasons founded The Royal Society, by Robert Lomas, Revised Edition –Published by Transworld, (21 May 2009) ISBN 978-0552158374

Essay 15 - Why Should a Quantum Physicist Take Freemasonry Seriously?

This essay I wrote at the request of the Master of the Lodge of Living Stones, Bro. Tony Baker, and was originally given at the Bristol Masonic Society in May 2012. Over the years Bro. Tony, who is a surgeon, and I, who am a physicist, have debated our different world views and whilst Tony has often described his viewpoint as arising from his faith that there is a force for order in the world, mine arises from my mathematical reasoning about the nature of that ordering force which makes the universe predictable. I have no faith, and no need of faith, since I deduce from experiment that ordering force must exist and I trust it completely.

As Masons we both describe this mysterious force as The Great Architect Of The Universe, but our approaches to TGAOFU are very different. Tony call his TGAOFU God whilst I call my TGAOFU the Laws of Physics. It is often perceived that there is no common ground between science and religion, but in my view Freemasonry occupies just such a common ground. It appears to me that it is a philosophy to help people, with any belief in an organized, purposeful, cosmos to understand the world, their place in it and themselves. The main area of overlap between Freemasonry and science is a shared use of symbols, and as I explain in this essay, the use of symbols in science came from inspiration derived from Freemasonry's teaching about symbols.

To join the Craft you must be able to express a belief in some form of Supreme Being. The nature of this belief is not probed but it is clear that without such a belief you cannot become a Freemason. A belief in a Supreme Force for Order within the Cosmos can take many forms and as I will explain it includes having a belief in the Laws of Physics.

I intend to consider the question posed in my title over three periods. The Past, discussing ideas from Freemasonry which influenced scientists before the twentieth century. The Present, which looks at ideas which grew out of the physics revolution of the early twentieth century. And finally the Future where I will look at how some the myths, metaphors and symbols of Freemasonry inspire my current thinking about the hidden mysteries of nature and science.

Part 1 - The Past

Must a Scientist be an Atheist? If you read only the works of Richard Dawkins then you might answer yes to this question. But you must remember Dawkins is a biologist, which is a form of science which is rather similar to bird-watching or stamp collecting. For physicists science begins with mathematics and ends with experiments. My generation of physicists was taught that there is no rhyme or reason in the behaviour of populations of small wave-like-objects, but we were shown how to became skilled manipulators of these tiny bits of matter and packets of energy, able to create a whole new range of technologies from our predictive equations. But the price we paid was the not just the loss of our sense of awe and wonder but a complete interdict on dabbling in spiritual metaphor which Dawkins has raised to a fine art.

We were treated as stupid heretics if we even considered that there might be interactions between reality and the intelligence of a conscious observer at the quantum level. And to suggest that we might even be able to understand such interactions was way beyond the pale. But that view is now changing as the role of consciousness in quantum events has been experimentally demonstrated.

One of my main heroes of science, Enrico Fermi, was a Mason before he became a great scientist, so he must have been able to express a belief in a form of Supreme Being. And from Newton down to Hawking a majority of the physicists whose work I admire have expressed views about the existence or otherwise of some sort of God, even if our use of the term God is a metaphor for the fundamental laws which all physicists believe to lie at the heart of creation..

Albert Einstein accepted the existence of a superior intelligence that he felt revealed itself in the harmony and beauty of nature. But he didn't extend this view to include a 'God who rewards and punishes the objects of his creation and whose purposes are modelled after our own'. [1] When he was asked directly to define God he wrote:

I'm not an atheist and I don't call myself a pantheist. I am in the position of a little child entering a huge library filled with books in many languages. The child knows someone must have written those books. It does not know how. It does not understand the language in which they are written. The child dimly suspects a mysterious order in the arrangement of the books but it doesn't know what it is. That, it seems to me, is the attitude of even the most intelligent human being toward God. We see the universe marvelously arranged and obeying certain laws but only dimly understand these laws. [2]

Werner Heisenberg, the man who discovered the Uncertainty Principle, made this forthright statement:

It may be argued that certain trends in Christian philosophy led to a very abstract concept of God, that they put God so far above the world that one began to consider the world without at the same time also seeing God in the world . . . then a new authority appeared which was completely independent of Christian religion or philosophy or of the Church, the authority of experience, of empirical fact . . . it spoke of two kinds of revelation of God. One was written in the Bible and the other was to be found in the book of nature. The holy scriptures had been written by man and were therefore subject to error, while nature was the immediate expression of God's intentions. [3]

When I became a Fellowcraft Freemason I was told it was my duty to study the hidden mysteries of nature and science so that I might better understand the mind of the Great Architect. This view has never been more clearly expressed than in the words of Heisenberg I have just quoted.

Erwin Schrödinger, the man who discovered the quantum wavefunction and invented the famous experiment with the cat in the box, was more explicit about the nature of God. He rejected the idea of a personal, interfering and vengeful god, but he also rejected the idea that scientists had to be atheists.

Let me briefly mention the notorious atheism of science . . . Science has to suffer this reproach again and again, but unjustly so. No personal god can form part of a world model that has only become accessible at the cost of removing everything personal from it. We know, when God is experienced, this is an event as real as an immediate sense perception or as one's own personality. Like them He must be missing in the space-time picture. I do not find God anywhere in space and time for God is spirit.[4]

The super-consciousness which I suspect might link a human mind to some cosmic intelligence is a deliberately cultivated state of being which Freemasonry calls 'awareness of the Centre'. The rituals of The Craft, and the support of a lodge, are intended to help individual Masons to achieve this state of insight. When they do, they know what Schrödinger called 'experiencing God as an immediate sense perception'.

Paul Direc, a Bristol man, who shared a Nobel Prize with Schrödinger and was a student of Bro. Sir James Jeans, said.

God is a mathematician of a very high order, and He used very advanced mathematics in constructing the universe.[5]

Richard Feynman, the discoverer of quantum electro-dynamics, explained how a sense of spiritual inspiration lay at the heart of his physics.

The same thrill, the same awe and mystery, comes again and again when we look at any question deeply enough. With more knowledge comes a deeper, more wonderful mystery, luring one on to penetrate deeper still. Never concerned that the answer may prove disappointing, with pleasure and confidence we turn over each new stone to find unimagined strangeness leading on to more wonderful questions and mysteries – certainly a grand adventure! . . . few unscientific people have this particular type of religious experience . . . This is not yet a scientific age.[6]

Fred Hoyle, too, came to the view that there is a cosmic intelligence that plays a part in the workings of the universe.

We learn in physics that non-living processes tend to destroy order, whereas intelligent control is particularly effective at producing order out of chaos. You might even say that intelligence shows itself most effectively in arranging things exactly as the origin of life requires. This point is so important that it is worth pausing to consider the very great difference that intelligence can make, not by thunder and lightning methods like Thor and his hammer, but by the subtlest of touches . . . Where is this intelligence situated? Exactly what does it do? What is its physical form? A generation or more of scientific consolidation is needed before risking a shot at such ambitious questions . . . Is intelligence outside the Earth inaccessibly remote or is it close enough to be contacted if only we knew how?[7]

I believe that Freemasonry may well have found a way of teaching its followers how to interact with this cosmic intelligence. But, of course, here is a crucial difference between Freemasonry and religion. The Craft imposes no supernatural theology upon how this interaction is to be understood.

Stephen Hawking, not noted for his spiritual sensitivity, when challenged in the letters page of *American Scientist* about being afraid to admit the existence of any form of Supreme Being, defended his physicist's sense of awe and freedom to interpret it, saying.

I thought I had left the question of the existence of a Supreme

Being completely open. It would be perfectly consistent with all we know to say that there was a Being who was responsible for the laws of physics. However, I think it could be misleading to call such a Being 'God' because this term is normally understood to have personal connotations which are not present in the laws of physics.[8]

Fred Hoyle's grudging acceptance of a cosmic intelligence is derived from his study of physics, as he said:

'God' is a forbidden word in science, but if we define an intelligence superior to ourselves as a deity, then we have arrived at two kinds – the intelligence . . . [of other evolved intelligent observers elsewhere in the cosmos] and the 'God' of the infinite future . . . In contemporary Western religions it is said that 'God' created the Universe and that 'God' can interfere with the Universe to suit himself. However, the Universe cannot interfere with 'God', so that, unlike the situation in science, action and reaction are not equal and opposite. This lopsidedness leads inevitably into a logical morass. One is impelled by such concepts to ask a question which turns out to be unanswerable; the question why the Universe should exist at all. As a distinguished modern theologian said 'What we cannot understand is that God who has no need of the world should have reason to create it,' but this morass is avoided when it is seen that 'God' exists only by virtue of the support received from the Universe.[9]

The modern science of physics, which Fred Hoyle practised at a high level, grew out of the work of John Wallis and Isaac Newton, who were in turn inspired by the injunction now given in the Second Degree of Freemasonry 'to study the hidden mysteries of nature and science to better know the Great Architect'.

As I will explain, Freemasonry, provides a route to spiritual understanding which is sometimes denied to devout religious believers but which appeals greatly to scientists and this is through its study and use of symbols.

The Platonic World View of Freemasonry

Analytical psychologist Carl Gustav Jung says that symbols speak to us of "things beyond the range of human understanding." They tap into a source of knowledge that is not normally accessible to our conscious minds. Jung said of such symbols

As the mind explores the symbol it is led to ideas that lie beyond the grasp of reason... Because there are innumerable things beyond the range of human understanding, we constantly use symbolic terms to represent concepts that we cannot define or fully comprehend.[10]

But what is this knowledge and where does it come from? This is a question which has haunted the human race for at least 2,500 years. The Greek philosopher Plato (427- 347 BCE) thought symbols came from a transcendental world of perfect and beautiful forms that only can be reached by the human soul. He believed that the most important human knowledge is recalled by the soul from the time before it was born. He said that if we consider our knowledge of equality we have no difficulty in deciding whether or not two people are equal in height. But they are never exactly the same height. It is always be possible to discover some difference—however minute—with a more careful, precise measurement. All the examples of equality we recognize in ordinary life only approach, but never quite attain, perfect equality. But since we realize truth from our experience, we must somehow know for sure what true equality is, even though we can never see it.[11] This kind of thinking led to the discovery of the symbols of geometry and mathematics, which opened up human understanding of reality.

All the symbols we can see around us are imperfect instances, but we have an inner knowledge of abstract things like truth, goodness, and beauty, as well as equality. These are the Platonic Forms, abstract entities that exist independently of the physical world. Plato said that ordinary objects are imperfect and changeable, but they faintly echo the perfect and immutable forms of their symbols. Many of the key symbols that have influenced human development are found among these Platonic Forms. Although we can never draw a perfect square, a perfect equilateral triangle or a perfect lozenge, we know what they are because our soul knows their symbolic, perfect form.

Plato argued we cannot possibly have knowledge of these perfect forms through any bodily experience, so our knowledge must be a memory that our souls carry from the transcendental place where the symbols exist in perfect form. Plato, whose ideas inspired part of the Masonic teachings, believed that the world is essentially intelligible, but it is our intellect, not our senses, that have the ultimate 'vision' of true being. We understand the world by the deep knowledge that is conveyed into our heart by symbols.

Both Plato and Jung speak of a reality that lies beyond normal human consciousness, which can only be reached through symbols. This symbolic knowledge has a spiritual or transcendental dimension, which has been the subject of Masonic study and teaching over the centuries.

John Wallis, an early Freemason, who became Savilian Professor of Geometry at Oxford in 1649, recognized that certain symbols could be utilized to stand in for real things, and could then be manipulated to explain, (or as scientists say "model") what was happening in the real world. When he passed this knowledge onto his brethren in the Royal Society, it opened up a whole new range of possibilities.

Wallis mentions a formal Masonic interest in the secret science of symbols and how they give insight into the hidden mysteries of nature. He had got into the habit of discussing his ideas at meetings whose purpose was to sensitize the brethren to the import of symbols. There was no better venue or audience for his ideas at that time than Brother Masons. This sensitization prepared Wallis for a great step forward by opening his mind to a new family of symbols. These are the symbols of mathematical equality, or as we know them today, the symbols of algebraic equations.

As a boy, Wallis had been fascinated by counting. This was how he was first introduced to the idea that symbols could potentially manipulate reality. In later life, he said about the experience:

Mathematics, at that time with us, were scarce looked on as academical studies, but rather mechanical—as the business of traders, merchants, seamen, carpenters, surveyors of lands and the like.[12]

His first encounter with representative symbols was at the hands of another Freemason and astrologer William Oughtred, the man who invented the slide rule. (The slide rule reduced multiplication and division to a simple mechanical manipulation of symbolic number positions, making it much easier to calculate the positions of the stars when casting a horoscope.) Wallis lived in Oughtred's house in Albury and received instruction in arithmetic. William Oughtred was a member of an early lodge of speculative Freemasons and the author of a book on arithmetic, *Clavis Mathematicae.* Oughtred introduced Wallis to the Masonic way of studying symbols. Wallis writes in his autobiography that he was so inspired by the inherent logic of Oughtred's book that he mastered its ideas within a couple of weeks. Before Wallis nobody had realized the great power inherent in the symbol of equality and the Masonic philosophy of balance and harmony which it symbolized.

The Power of Equality

There is an incredible mystery hidden within the simple equations that we all learn at school. This symbolic power of equations comes from two key factors:

- A symbol can be used to represent something which is real, like the speed a stone falls to the ground or the number of gulps of trapped air a man can take in a diving bell without running out of oxygen.

- The equality described by an equation is total, absolute, and uncompromising.

When John Wallis began to discover the full power of the "=" symbol, he had the benefit of Masonic training to sensitize him to the two parts of this symbol's revelation. Freemasonic sensitization suggests that the "=" symbol looks like the two pillars " ‖ " laid horizontally and meaning "is equal to." (you could say rotated through an angle of 90 degree or the fourth part of a circle)

In 1656, Wallis wrote a book called *Arithmetica infinitorum* where he drew on this relationship between the Level and the Square to work out the value of π. (a number that relates the diameter of a circle to its circumference). The challenge of figuring out this transcendental property of a circle from a series of counting symbols laid out in a logical order intrigued him.

In his *Treatise on Algebra,* Wallis explained how symbols can reveal matters which are otherwise inaccessible to human understanding. He said that a symbolic equation had the power to uncover the mechanisms of nature. The name he chose for accessing this hidden power was "algebra." He took the word from the Arabic, and it means "to bring together."

In his *Treatise on Algebra,* Wallis discovered ways to evaluate equations which would later be used by Newton in his fundamental work on physics.

The newly formed Royal Society, of which Wallis was a founding member, was a potent package. It brought together a lively group of thinkers, many of them Freemasons, pre-sensitized to symbols, and gave them money, encouragement, and a journal to share knowledge. Without this freedom to study the works of The Great Architect Newton's ideas would never have been published. Less than a generation earlier, Galileo had been persecuted for daring to suggest the Earth might revolve around the sun. Yet only fifty years later Newton was able to write about knowing the Mind of God through the symbolic equations which

The Great Architect used to control the movements of the heavens.

To become a Fellowcraft Freemason you have to admit in front of the whole lodge that the earth goes round the sun. The tools Newton discovered grew from an alliance between the Masonic symbols of geometry and the newly discovered analytic symbols of algebra. Newton said of his symbolic insight into the mind of God:

Have we any idea of the substance of God? We know him only by his most wise and excellent contrivances of things, and final causes; we admire him for his perfections; but we reverence and adore him on account of his dominion; for we adore him as his servants; and a god without dominion, providence, and final causes is nothing else but Fate and Nature. Blind metaphysical necessity, which is certainly the same always and everywhere, could produce no variety of things. All that diversity of natural things which we find suited to different times and places could arise from nothing but the ideas and will of a Being necessarily existing. Thus, the diligent student of science, the earnest seeker of truth, is led, as through the courts of a sacred Temple, wherein, at each step, new wonders meet the eye, till, as a crowning grace, they stand before a Holy of Holies, and learn that all science and all truth are one which hath its beginning and its end in the knowledge of Him whose glory the heavens declare, and whose handiwork the firmament showeth forth.[13]

This comment by Newton shows that he feels the symbols of mathematics, which enabled him to understand the movements of the heavens, are thoughts that come directly from The Great Architect, not something invented by men.

Newton also received symbolic teaching from Freemasons which guided him as well. When he first went to Cambridge University as an undergraduate he seemed odd to his fellow students. He had no interest in socializing and spent all his time thinking and making notes about algebraic symbols. When the Black Death swept through Cambridge, his degree studies were interrupted and he spent a year at his home in Lincolnshire to avoid catching the plague, sitting and thinking in solitary isolation.

His notebooks show that during his first term at Cambridge he bought a copy of Freemason William Lily's book *Christian Astrology*. He struggled to understand it because it involved two branches of symbolic reasoning known as geometry and trigonometry. This pushed him to study the writings of Lily's fellow Mason, John Wallis. Newton's student notes show that Wallis became his early inspiration:

About the beginning of my mathematical studies, the works of our celebrated countryman, Dr. Wallis, fell into my hands...[14]

Wallis inspired Newton's interest in arithmetic, alchemy, astrology, and methods of arithmetic calculation. After reading Wallis, Newton felt inspired to look at the works of Euclid. (The Propositions of Euclid form part of the ritual explanations and myths about Euclid form a key part of the Masonic canon.) Reading Wallis also inspired Newton to read and absorb the symbolic ideas in Oughtred's *Clavis Mathematicae.*

Many people think that Newton became a Freemason when he joined The Royal Society in 1671. It seems likely, as it was an organization dominated by speculative Freemasons. However, I have been unable to find any record of an initiation, even though Newton's notebooks show that his interest in symbolic thinking grew rapidly after mixing with men from the Royal Society.

Newton first met with the members of the Royal Society in 1664 while he was still a student. From then on he took a special interest in Solomon's Temple, writing many unpublished, notes about this topic, more than he wrote about mathematics or science.[15] Solomon's Temple is a subject of special interest to us Freemasons, because it is the underlying myth used in the Masonic method of sensitizing members to the hidden meaning of symbols and the power of symbolic buildings to represent our souls.. Masonic myth says Solomon's Temple was inspired by God, whom we call *The Grand Geometrician of the Universe.*

Newton became a fellow of Trinity College, Cambridge, in 1667, and Lucasian Professor of Mathematics two years later. Between 1673 and 1683 he gave a series of lectures on algebra and the theory of equations, but much of his spare time was taken up studying in Solomon's Temple as he tried to understand the method of thinking used by *The Grand Geometrician*.[16] His work on equations extended Wallis's use of the equals "=" symbol, and was published in 1707 in a book called The *Universal Arithmetic*.

During 1692 he corresponded with John Wallis and discussed ideas about a form of symbolic representation which he turned into his greatest work on the reality of nature.[15] The method of symbolic manipulation he discovered is now known as the calculus, but then was called the method fluxions. It combined the symbolic visualization system of Euclid with Wallis's representation of physical quantities as algebraic symbols. Newton drew on the Masonic idea of God as the Grand Geometrician of the Universe to bring Euclid's system of graphic symbols together with the mathematical analysis made possible by algebraic symbols. He published this work during 1687 as *Principia Mathematica*. It was a landmark step towards understanding the universe.

Newton's discovery of the secrets of equality gave a totally new view of how the Universe is controlled and ordered. The French mathematician Lagrange described the *Principia* as:

The greatest production of the human mind, and said he felt dazed at such an illustration of what man's intellect might be capable. In describing the effect of his own writings and those of Laplace it was a favorite remark of his that Newton was not only the greatest genius that had ever existed, but he was also the most fortunate, for as there is but one universe, it can happen but to one man in the world's history to be the interpreter of its laws.[18]

Newton's understanding came from his study of Masonic symbolism. The innate power of the symbols to influence human minds can be seen by the way this Masonic knowledge affected the thought processes of others as Newton shared it. In particular there was a dispute between the German philosopher Gottfried Leibnitz and Newton about who discovered calculus.

What is less well known is that both Newton and Leibniz were exposed to the same symbolic teaching by Freemasons of the Royal Society. Newton through his association with John Wallis, and his reading of Lily and Oughtred. Leibniz through a protracted correspondence with Bro. Sir Robert Moray, the Freemason who founded the society.

The symbolic mix of geometric insight and algebraic analysis which is the calculus, appeared simultaneously to two men as if it had been fully formed in another place and was just waiting for a chance to manifest in human minds.

Masonic teaching offers a means of accessing the place where symbols are eternally present. This place is called by some physicists the Platonic Heaven and is derived from Plato's discovery of the perfect forms.

Wallis, Lily, and Oughtred introduced Newton to a tradition which has since become commonplace among modern scientists. Wallis and Newton believed that pure symbols arose from the mind of God, existed before the world began, and would endure long after the world had passed into oblivion.

Part 2 - The Present

Implicit in this eternal world view is the idea that for a mathematical theorem to be discovered it must already exist before any human thinks about it. I have previously mentioned that this idea of a transcendental world of absolute symbolic forms was proposed by the Greek philosopher Plato (427-347 BCE).

Plato believed that we have genuine knowledge of truth, goodness, and beauty as well as of equality, even though we perceive only imperfect instances in the real world. Things of this sort he called Platonic Forms, abstract entities that exist independently of the sensible world. Ordinary objects are imperfect and changeable, but they faintly copy the perfect and immutable Forms. Many of the Platonic shapes, such as the square, the equilateral triangle, the circle, the pentangle, and the heptangle appear in the Masonic set of symbols.

Roger Penrose, a committed scientific Platonist, writes about this idea:

The Platonic viewpoint is an immensely valuable one. It tells us to be careful to distinguish the precise mathematical entities from the approximations that we see around us in the world of physical things. Moreover, it provides us with the blueprint according to which modern science has proceeded. Scientists will put forward models of the world—or, rather, of certain aspects of the world—and these models may be tested against previous observation and against the results of carefully designed experiment.

If the model itself is to be assigned any kind of 'existence,' then this existence is located within the Platonic world of mathematical forms. Of course, one might take a contrary viewpoint: namely that the model is itself to have existence only within our various minds, rather than to take Plato's world to be in any sense absolute and 'real.' Yet, there is something important to be gained in regarding mathematical structures as having a reality of their own. For our individual minds are notoriously imprecise, unreliable, and inconsistent in their judgments. The precision, reliability, and consistency that are required by our scientific theories demand something beyond any one of our individual (untrustworthy) minds. In mathematics, we find a far greater robustness than can be located in any particular mind. Does this not point to something outside ourselves, with a reality that lies beyond what each individual can achieve?

The philosophy of eternal and perfect symbols which underlies the scientific method of answering questions about reality gives rise to the term "Re-search." As a scientist, when Penrose conducts Re-search he is repeating a search, which any individual could repeat independently, to discover a truth about the symbolic nature of reality which can be found by anyone prepared to interact with the Platonic symbols, which is of course, one of the aims of Freemasonry.

This concept of re-search was formalized during World War II, when scientists working for the Allies, in particular Leo Szilard and Albert Einstein in the U.S.[20] and Neils Bohr in the U.K., realized that a weapon of immense destructive power already existed within the realms of symbolic Truth. The implication of this thought was that a frightful weapon was sitting, waiting to cooperate with first bold searcher to discover it and let it help them to win the war. That searcher could be on either side, as basic work on nuclear instability had been carried out by Heisenberg but ignored by Hitler. In the U.K., work on material preparation for a ballistic-impact uranium bomb was already well underway at the Nobel explosive works in Porth Madog, North Wales, under the secret patronage of the MAUD committee.[21] But a real fear was shared by Albert Einstein and Neils Bohr, that this fearsome weapon was sitting, unprotected, in the heaven of the Platonic symbols just waiting to be accessed and used.

Szilard and Einstein wrote to President Roosevelt urging him to devote all the U.S.'s scientific talent to searching for this atom bomb. They warned that the consequences of Hitler getting to it first would be catastrophic.[22] Roosevelt, himself a Freemason, took their warning seriously and set up The Manhattan Project. It brought together the organizational and logistic skills of General Leslie Groves and the inspired scientific leadership of Dr J. Robert Oppenheimer in the remote desert site of Los Alamos, to exploit the reality of nuclear fission which was demonstrated by Bro. Enrico Fermi . The result was two symbolic discoveries, two different types of atom bomb, one based on uranium (Little Boy) and one based on a previously unknown Platonic element, plutonium (Fat Boy). Both bombs worked and were deployed over Japanese cities. Nobody now questions the idea that there are symbolic scientific entities just waiting in the Platonic heaven to be discovered by explorers who know how to reach those realms. The atomic bomb is harrowing proof of this.

Part 3 - The Future

Here, to close this essay I will give a few examples of how the myth and symbolism of Freemasonry helps me as a scientist to understand some of the thoughts which pass through the mind of the Great Architect.

The Divine Spark

Both the Craft and physics agree that symbols are eternal things sitting in a Platonic heaven waiting for us to discover them and their power.

Science and Freemasonry both set out to sensitise and imprint symbols in the minds of their followers by ritual exposure. Over time the imprinted symbols become a focus for meditative power and a means of increasing depth of understanding. The intense schooling in mathematics, undergone by the scientist is even more demanding and severe than the Initiatory ritual discipline imposed by The Craft on its Candidates. But both paths increase the Initiate's power to reason and understand reality. So how does Freemasonry inspire me to think about the future of science?

Freemasonry tells me that deep within me, at the centre of my being, is a divine spark which allows me link with the Great Architect. In his book The Meaning of Masonry, Bro Walter Wilmshurst, the founder of my own lodge wrote

The Fellowcraft degree involves not merely the cleansing and control of the mind, but a full comprehension of our inner constitution, of the more hidden mysteries of our nature and of spiritual psychology. In this degree it is that our attention is called to the fact that the Mason who has attained proficiency in this grade has been enabled to discover a sacred symbol, placed in the centre of the building, and alluding to the Great Architect. The building alluded to is not the edifice we meet in, but is our own selves, and that the sacred symbol exists at the centre of ourselves. At the depths of our own being, there resides nothing other than a spark of the Great Architect, immanent within us.

Over the old temples of the Mysteries was written the injunction "Man, know thyself, and thou shalt know the universe and God." Happy then is the Mason who has so far purified and developed his own nature as to realize in its fulness the meaning of the "sacred symbol" of the second degree, and found the Great Architect present within himself.

And this beautiful idea of a small part of our inner self being able to link with the laws of nature ties in directly with the teachings of quantum physics.

Wilmshurst claims there is a small spark in my soul that is able to interact with the Great Architect and help carry out the Divine Plan. As a physicist I have to agree with him. There is an unexplained, and widely unacknowledged, implication of quantum theory. For an observation to take place, so that a fixed past is assigned to an object, an intelligent mind has to interact with the measurement. Fred Hoyle explains it from the scientist's viewpoint:

Certainty comes in an individual experiment only after it has actually been done, and certainty comes only by observing the outcome of a particular experiment, with our consciousness telling us the result. . . . It comes as something of a shock to find one's consciousness being involved in this way, and many scientists, while accepting the basic ideas of quantum physics, try to avoid the involvement of consciousness by what seems to me to be a deception.[23]

The words may be different but the implication is identical. Wilmshurst called that consciousness, the Divine Spark. The deception referred to by Hoyle, by which scientists avoid thinking about this Divine Spark, is The Copenhagen Interpretation. Throughout his life Hoyle struggled with its implications for quantum physics, as Einstein did before him. Both of them concluded that consciousness and intention, that is to say intelligence (or, speaking Masonically, the Divine Spark which implements the Divine Plan) has a role in determining the outcomes of observations.

Quantum physics tells me that when deciding what to observe I can change the nature of the reality I am observing. By observing I interact with reality and modify it for ever and throughout all space-time. But, most importantly, there are choices in this process which are affected by my intentions as an observer.

By deciding to make an observation today we might make quite drastic changes to the very distant past of the cosmos, our very distant past and the distant past of all other species of intelligent observers which might exist out of range of our light-speed-limited perceptions. And if we can do this, we can also be affected by other entities involved in the same instantaneous process.

Since matter, in the form of intelligent observers, developed the ability to become curious about itself it has had an impact on the history and development of the universe. Curiosity has driven humans to make observations of the earliest phases of the Universe and in doing so has forced a particular form of reality on the past as quantum physics says that the past of the physical universe was not resolved and fixed until it was observed by minds which desired to nurture consciousness.

So by studying the nature of the divine spark and learning to know myself, I can also learn about the nature of quantum wavefunction collapse. But now let us move on to another symbol of the Great Architect. The circle containing an equilateral triangle.

The Triangular Mystery of the Quark's Domestic Life.

Just as there is a Divine Spark within my consciousness which cannot be separated from my living mind, so there are strange sub-atomic particles, which cannot be separated, hidden in the centre of the protons and neutrons which make up the nucleus of every atom. All atoms consist mainly of empty spare. They are rather like miniature solar systems. At the centre, instead of a sun, there is a nucleus consisting of a number of protons, which carry a single unit of electric charge, and neutrons which do not have any electric charge. Around this central nucleus electrons circle like orbiting planets. The simplest element is hydrogen, which has one proton, no neutrons and one electron orbiting its lone proton. The most complex naturally-occurring element on earth is uranium which usually has 92 protons and 145 neutrons, all clumped together in its nucleus and 92 electrons buzzing round it in orbit.

But do the elemental particles also have a Divine spark within them? If you had asked me that question in in 1964, when I was finishing my A levels I would have said "certainly not" But had you asked me again in 1972, when I was freshly doctored, and I would have answered "I think so."

By then I had a strong mathematical basis for believing there were even smaller particles than protons and neutron. The theory of these sub-atomic particles had been proposed by a Bristol physicist Paul Dirac, the concept developed by Gell-Mann & Zweig, (who named the quark after a quote in Finnegan's Wake "three quarks for Master Mark" as he liked the sound of the word and it takes three quarks to make a boson). Predicting the behavour of quarks was made possible using an ingenious set of geometric diagrams discovered by Richard Feynman after reading Euclid's classic work on analytical geometry. (Incidentally Feynman married a girl from Yorkshire and once played the bongo drums in the Queen's Head pub in Ripponden, W Yorks. but that's another story). And the first quarks were found experimentally at the new laboratory called Fermi Lab, which was created as a memorial to Bro. Enrico Fermi.

Bro. Fermi's qualities as a scientist also sum up the qualities expected of a Fellow Craft Freemason. His colleague Herbert Anderson said of him.

Fermi was always eager to learn. He was always grateful when he found out something new. What he learned he felt he should enrich. Having enriched what he learned he felt he should teach to others. Thus, he prepared the fertile ground out of which arose the new solutions and new ideas which kept his subject bright, fresh, and exciting.

To explore the mysteries of nature with Enrico Fermi was always a great adventure and a thrilling experience. He had a sure way of starting off in the right direction, of setting aside the irrelevancies, of seizing all the essentials and proceeding to the core of the matter. The whole process of wresting from nature her secrets was for Fermi an exciting sport which he entered into with supreme confidence and great zest.

It is not my intention to teach you the theory of bosons, fermions and quark interaction in this essay but I suggest you look at how Feynman adapted the geometry of Euclid, which we study in our Masonic lectures, in order to simplify the understanding of quark interactions and created mathematical diagrams of three quarks within a boson (such as a proton or a neutron) showing how they form a triangle with a circle - the traditional Masonic symbol for the Deity.

The Life-Giving Mystery of Darkness Visible.

The Sun is the most visible source of light in our world and its importance is acknowledged in the ritual as we acknowledge whenever we form at lodge.

As the sun raises in the East to open and enliven the day so it the worshipful master placed the East to open his lodge to employ and instruct his brethren in Freemasonry.

But what is the hidden mystery of nature and science which enables the sun to pour enormous amounts of light and energy into the dark space surrounding it and so warm the earth to a liveable temperature?

Before the sun formed, about 4.5 billion years ago, the space it now occupies was dark and cold. and contained wisps of it the most common element in the universe - hydrogen. Basic hydrogen has one proton at the centre of its atom and one electron orbiting around the proton. There is nothing simpler in the whole of creation and left to itself is is not a showy element so you can't really see is when is it a thinly spread gas in the dark and cold of outer space. However get enough hydrogen in one place and gravity pulls it into a ball which grows and pulls in more hydrogen. As it is increasingly compressed under its own weight it starts to heat up (in the same way as if you compress air in a hand pump to blow up the tyres of your bicycle you will notice the pump gets hot). As the ball of dark, black hydrogen sucks in more mass to compress the gas, first the electrons get stripped away from the protons, and form a sort of common cloud of electrons and then the quarks within the proton get irritated by all the heavy, positively charged protons being crushed together when they want to fly apart. Now the darkness starts to become visible as the pressure changes the hydrogen into helium (which has two electrons orbiting a nucleus of two protons and two neutrons)

A proton has two **up** quarks and one **down** quark forming a balanced triangle of forces. But a neutron, which is about the same size and weight as a proton, but has no charge, so doesn't push surrounding protons or neutrons away from it.. A neutron is made from two **down** quarks and one **up** quark forming another balanced triangle of forces. Now if you now apply enough pressure a plasma of protons you can make some **up** quarks flip and become **down** quarks. Cram enough protons and neutrons together and some neutrons will stick to a free protons to form a new nucleus. But as the **up** quark flips to become a **down** quark it throws out the charge of the proton in the form a positron (the particle discovered by Paul Dirac)

So if we take four atoms of hydrogen we start with four protons and four electrons. From this we can make one atom of helium, which has two protons, two neutrons and two electrons. During this mystical conversion we have created two positrons and discarded two free electrons. When a electron collides with positron, which is its antiparticle, then all the energy of two electrons and the two anti-electrons is radiated in the form of neutrinos and photons of light and heat which brighten and enliven the day. And without that process we would not be here.

So to sum up. Why do I take Freemasonry seriously?

Because it teaches me three important lessons.

1. Symbols can convey messages which transcend and exceed the limitations of words.

2. There is a commonly accessible transcendental region where all the symbolic knowledge about reality lies waiting to be discovered.

3. Individuals can work together to understand and access this symbolic repository and use the knowledge they gain to understand, manipulate and contribute to reality, so giving their lives purpose. And by working together their sum is greater than their parts.

Freemasonry has been sustained by inspiring thinkers, who in their turn have created societies to illuminate the hidden mysteries of nature and science by the power of symbolic reasoning. Brethren we are lucky to be the guardians of such an inspiring tradition.

Essay 16 - What Should Freemasonry Do?

Freemasonry has a problem and that problem is a function of the mismatch between its infrastructure, its age profile and its current membership.

Its membership is aging and is dying out quicker than it is being replaced. For the first generation in nearly 300 hundred year of existence English Freemasonry is declining in membership. And all its history has only ever taught it to expand. Its rank system and its regional organization is based on an historical expectation of growth, which as I will show, can no longer relied on.

To see the nature of the problem look at this graph. Its show a steady increase in membership until 1981 followed a sharp downturn. But this is only part of the problem.

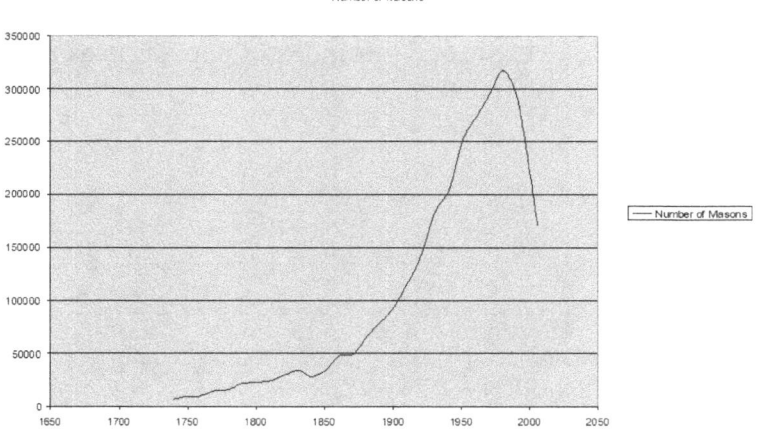

Figure 1 Number of Subscribing Members Plotted against the Year

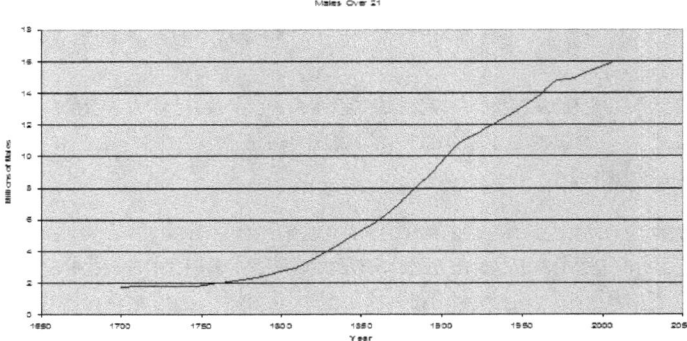

Figure 2 Number of eligible Males in the English Population

This has happened during a period of steady growth in the number of males aged 21 or over as shown by the above graph. This mismatch indicates a clear change in attitude.

The degree of variation in popularity can be calculated by working out the proportion of males who choose to join Freemasonry. I have expressed this index of popularity as the ratio of Freemasons per 1000 males.

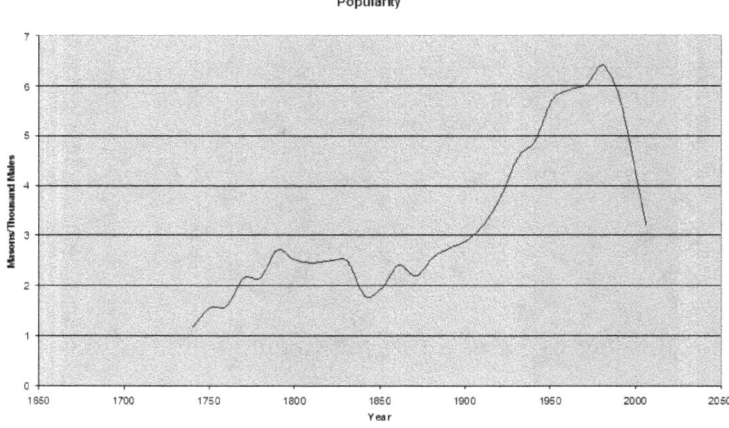

Figure 3 Index of Popularity of Freemasonry from 1700 - 2006

Figure 3 shows the market penetration of Freemasonry in terms for Masons per thousand males in the population of England from the year 1700 until 2006. The average market penetration over the whole of Freemasonry's pubic life in England has been about 3 Masons per thousand eligible males but this figure is heavily weighted by the success Freemasonry during the twentieth century.

A sudden upsurge began in 1841 and grew to a peak in 1981. Since then it has been declining back towards what appears to be its more normal level of 2.4 Masons per thousand eligible males.

During the period 1911 to 1981 the average market penetration was 5.07 Masons per thousand eligible males - over double the historical equilibrium level of penetration. During this period 5,008 new lodges were formed. This graph shows the rate of lodge creation.

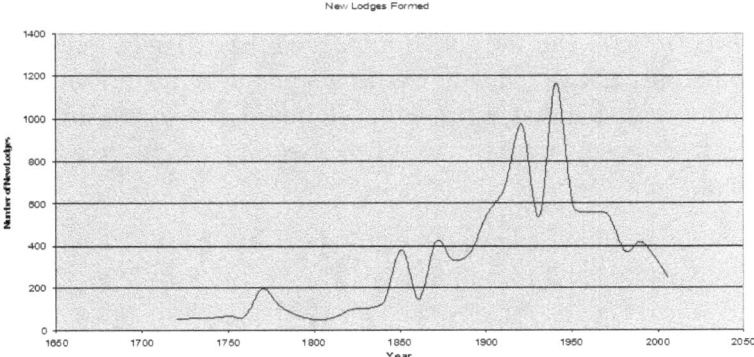

Figure 4 Number of New Lodges Formed in Each Year

Let me put Freemasonry's problem in context.

From 1700 until 1981 Freemasonry was a expanding organization. It's average yearly growth in membership up to 1981 was 18% per annum.

If we look at the highly successful period from 1911 to 1931 its average yearly increase in membership reached 25% per year. During this period 1,668 new lodges were formed.

There was a slow down in recruitment from 1941 to 1981 to a rate of 11.84% increase in members per annum despite a steadily increasing level of market penetration, averaging at 5.8 Masons per thousand eligible males. The number of new lodges formed was 2,883.

These figures seem to confirm the idea that the two world wars encouraged membership of Freemasonry as returning servicemen looked for a way of replacing the comradeship they had known in the services but the upward trend in popularity began sixty years before World War I.

The period during and after the two world wars was the golden age of expansion for Freemasonry. It's impact continued to be felt until the 1980's. But the social impact of the 1914-18 and the 1939-45 wars only accelerated an existing social trend. And this rapid growth in popularity continued until the beginning of the 1980's, long after the social aftermath of the Second World War had ceased.

However, in the last thirty years there has been a reversion to an earlier, lower, level of popularity.

Between 1981 and 1991 a major change happened to Freemasonry. There was a slower percentage yearly increase in eligible males and the market penetration ratio fell from the peak of 6.41 to 5.7 Masons per thousand eligible males. This drop of 11% in market penetration was partly counteracted by an increase in population but it still resulted in the first reduction in overall membership in the history of the Order. The membership fell by 8.42% and the direct result was what can only be described as a "churning of lodges".

Despite an 8.42% decline in membership 374 new lodges were formed. This suggests that there was an organizational pressure to create new lodges, which of course in a situation of declining membership, results in multiple lodge membership and is a way of increasing income for the central organization which is facing severe reductions in fee income.

This phenomenon can best be illustrated by plotting a graph of the ratio of extra members of Freemasonry to the number of new lodges formed to contain them. You would normally expect this to be positive, indicating that as the Order grew it created new lodges to serve the expanding membership. And from 1701 to 1981 this was largely true, the only exception being around the time of the Union of the Antients and the Moderns when many lodges were erased or combined into a new roll of lodges and there was a lot of moving between lodges. At this time a new lodge was formed for every 42 members who moved from erased lodges but as Figure 1 shows, there was little impact on the increasing number of men wishing to be made Masons.

But after 1981 the true lunacy of "lodge churning" can be seem. By 1991 a new lodge was being formed for every 65 members who left the Order, either by death or resignation.

Between 1991 and 2007 that figure has risen to a new lodge for every 492 members who leave the order and Freemasonry has warranted 660 new lodges over that period.

The rate of change in membership has been -42% in a period when the eligible male population has increased by 3.81%. Yet new lodges are still being created. This continuing creation of new lodges suggests an organization which is in denial about the extent of its decline.

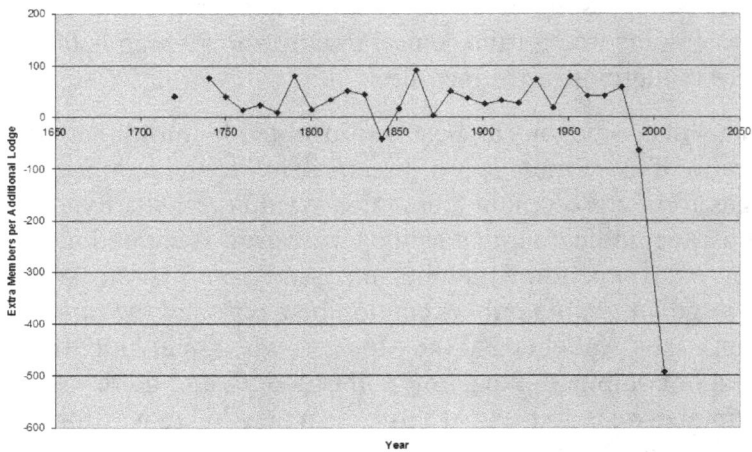

Ratio of Extra Members / New Lodges

Figure 5 Ratio of Increase in Membership to New Lodges Created

Looking over the figures I suspect that the recruitment impacts of the two world wars have now died out of the system and the surge of recruitment in sixties and seventies, which resulted from the baby-boomers being drawn in by their fathers and uncles, is aging. It seems that Masonry is settling back to its historical market penetration level of about 2.5 Masons per thousand eligible males. My analysis also suggests that the decline is not yet complete. When it is, what is left of Freemasonry will be a smaller organization needing fewer lodges and fewer Masonic halls.

If its infrastructure is to survive it needs to adjust its organization to fit its membership and funding levels. This implies fewer meeting places and more co-operation between lodges in sharing premises which can also act as local commercial function halls. A much smaller hierarchy is all that is needed to support the reduced organization.

The failure to appeal to the present and next generation needs to be addressed and ways of promoting a positive message about Freemasonry have to be developed and I'm not sure how we do it.

The decline in membership, to what has historically been the norm, suggests that Freemasonry will survive in a smaller form. But as it becomes smaller there will be far fewer opportunities for elaborate systems of rank. Such a smaller, flatter organization may not appeal to the current senior membership who have become 'rulers' of the Craft during a time of endless growth and bounty. I suspect the years of decline have further to run before the Order stabilizes at some new lower level, probably around 95,000 - 100,000. This prediction indicates that there will be a further decline of about 40% in both membership and funds before the rate of recruitment matches the rate of mortality.

What is clear from this analysis is that unless corporate Freemasonry starts to plan for a graceful decline it will sleep-walk to its death. But then again this may be no bad thing. It would allow a return to small local lodges, meeting in hired rooms in pubs, providing a format for meeting like-minded individuals who are interested in the social and spiritual rewards of Freemasonry, rather than seeking an alternative route to the acclaim which most people reap from success in normal life.

Freemasonry has been a a much greater force for spiritual and social improvement when it has drawn from a smaller group within the population. Perhaps the idea of a small, select band, keeping the message of The Craft alive, is what it needs to look at – as a model for the future.

Essay 17 - Whither or Wither Freemasonry?

In 2003, as the opening sentence of a book, I wrote "Freemasonry is dying!"

I went to say that:

"For most people life is far more complicated than it was just a generation ago. We work harder and we have more disposable income.

Long-term commitments are usually avoided at all costs. In an age when employment comes packaged as a series of renewable contracts and even marriage is out of vogue, it is not surprising that men no longer queue up to sign on for a lifetime of acting out odd-ball rituals in a local hall with no windows. A candidate for the Craft is expected to enter into a life-long relationship with a lodge before learning what Freemasonry is. They are given no advance warning of what they will be expected to do, or what benefit it will be to them. It is little wonder that the Grand Lodges who govern Freemasonry around the world are having difficulty in selling a proposition that does not meet any of the normal criteria of a marketable product.

An obvious question is 'does the demise of this secretive Order really matter?' Maybe Freemasonry should be allowed to quietly wither away."

Perhaps Freemasonry should die out and perhaps it will. As I showed in the statistical analysis of a previous essay, Freemasonry is declining in popularity. It surged to historically high levels of market penetration, between 1850 and 1980. During that period it went from an historical position of attracting about two men for every thousand in the eligible population to a peak of at least six men in a thousand joining the Craft. Since then it has declined to around 3 men per thousand and is still plummeting. It may stabilize at the historical mean of two per thousand but there is no certainty in this forecast. What is certain is that the periods of rapid growth, the periods when over a thousand new lodges were warranted year on year, have gone, probably for ever. Yet at the peak of this expansion there were an hundred new members for each newly created lodge, and the attitudes developed during this time remain in force. Freemasonry has been slow to adapt to its new position. At the present time it is losing 500 members for every new lodge which is warranted. So why is it still creating lodges? It seems to me to be either a policy of despair or a denial of reality. As more older members die and fewer new members come forward there are less brethren to shoulder the running costs. The number of new lodges formed each year peaked around 1948, when it hit an historical high of 1150 in one year. The rate of lodge creation has since declined to around 300 per year but overall the number of viable lodges is falling. Freemasonry needs to become a smaller and more focused organization. Creating swaths of new lodges, drawn entirely from the dwindling pool of existing members, makes no sense.

What is going on? Why is there a lemming-like rush to create more and more lodges for less and less subscribers. Could it be that Freemasonry, with its hierarchical structure ossified in the attitudes of the 1940's, knows of no other way to secure the loyalty of its older members? Do they really need the ego-fix of being a founder member to increase their pinny size? Will the tottering undemocratic structure of UGLE topple without the affiliation fees that lodge creation generates? To hold onto its existing brethren Freemasonry needs to provide incentives and unfortunately the incentive which most attracts aging, retired Masonic single-issue fanatics is also perhaps the most effective deterrent for potential new members. I talk of course about the so-called "Masonic Career Path" and the thrill of becoming a "Past" holder of an office you never held in the first place.

It is an over-complication which has grown out of the ancient Masonic teaching that in order to learn you must progress through the various offices of the lodges, learning something about yourself, your brethren and the world as you do so. You start as a Candidate - blind, shackled and fearful as you are led to the door of the lodge to be challenged by the outer guard. Having faced up to your emotions you progress as a student, learning how develop your intellect and to confront your ego's fear of death to emerge from the process as Master Mason.

But then you must learn how to teach, as only by passing on your understanding are you able to truly internalize the lessons of your various stages of Masonic apprenticeship.

You guard the outer door of the lodge and challenge the new Candidates, you present the sharp point of the dagger to the naked breast of the newly admitted. You share with your brother deacon the tasks of escorting and guiding apprentices and fellowcrafts as they circle the lodge on their path to Mastership. Then you take responsibility for a region of the lodge, beginning in the warm glow of the south, when the sun is at its meridian where you decide when to call the brethren from labour to refreshment and when to resume their labours. As you continue to grow, you become strong enough to face up to the mysteries of shadow and move to oversee the west, where at the dread hour of departing light you reassure the brethren that the hireling is paid and all will get their due. Then as you learn to master your fear of darkness you are ready to move through the drear blackness of the ignorant north to take your seat in the radiant east, and now you attempt to instruct your brethren in Freemasonry. Here it becomes your duty to pass on what you have learned on your journey to those who have not yet completed their pilgrimage. And so you finally end up, sitting at the left hand of the Right Worshipful Master, having reached your goal which is the office of Silence, and are now known as a Past Master. There you can sit and reflect on what you have learned about yourself and observe the progress of those who follow on, perhaps occasionally offering a helpful word of encouragement, perhaps occasionally gaining a new insight. At one time that state was the highest aspiration of a spiritually inclined Mason.

Now we get to the crux of the problem. During its period of rapid expansion Freemasonry over-promoted many of its members and moved them into offices before they were spiritually mature enough. It ended up with a surfeit of Past Masters who were unprepared for the sage-like state of reflective silence they should have been aspiring to. Having dipped deeply into the pool of ex-military men, between 1910 and 1950, the Order found its growing ranks of Past Masters wanted a continuing system of promotion, so it invented one. As the Order took on a greater proportion of the male population, it took in many who were ambitious beyond the rewards which the Craft traditionally offered. This new and expanded body of brothers were not content reflect on the knowledge of themselves that their progressive initiation had afforded them, they wanted a system of Masonic acclimation to celebrate their preferment and advertise their advancement. And so the top-heavy system of provincial and grand lodge honours was born. During the golden years of rapid growth there were enough submissive cannon fodder coming forward to support, and pay for, this system and lodges proliferated. But now times have changed. Now we must recruit young men who have been taught to think for themselves and have no interest in being subservient.

Traditionally Freemasonry has been attractive to a small proportion of the population who are interested in knowing and understanding themselves. It has offered a practical and incorporeal way to develop your spirit, and has managed largely to keep clear of the dogmatic traps of organized religion. Indeed, at the present period, when the public images of religion are being dominated by fundamentalist bigots, Freemasonry could reap enormous benefits by offering its alternative tradition of progressive initiation, democratic preferment and inherent toleration of differing views. Instead it is saddled with an overbearing post-military hierarchy of meaningless obsequies, enforced by a jobs-worth smalled-mindedness which drives away the younger generation who are not prepared to play such silly games.

Indeed my own indifference to the annual ritual of installation and my refusal to be installed in the chair of any English lodge, stems not from any distaste for the ceremony's basic message or import, but from a disgust at the travesty of enforced subservience which has been made an essential part of it under the United Grand Lodge of England (UGLE). By calling on every Master Elect of every private Lodge in England to take an oath in open lodge, to be totally obedient to each and every edict of the United Grand Lodge of England, no matter how stupid, short-sighted or patently silly such an edit may be, is a violation of the democratic essence of Freemasonry.

In the latter part of the twentieth century there was considerable pressure on UGLE, from non-Masons, to remove the traditional penalty, "of having my throat cut across, my tongue torn from its roots and my body buried in the rough sands of the sea whence the tide passes twice in the course of a natural day", which all Freemason's throughout the world once took. Despite the assurance given within the Ancient Charges of Freemasonry "that it is not in the power of any man or body of men to make any alteration or innovation in the body of Masonry," these traditional symbolic penalties, dating back hundreds of years and never carried out, were dropped under the pressure of non-Masonic bodies who found them distasteful.

So we know it is possible to change the ritual to remove what are deemed to be old-fashioned, distasteful and demeaning oaths. However a much more serious oath of disloyalty to the wishes brethren of one's one lodge remains. Why?

When the UGLE was formed in 1813, and the two rival Grand Lodges of the Ancients and the Moderns were brought together under the iron fist of the Duke of Sussex, this new oath was added to the Masonic ritual of Installation. Every prospective Master had to agree to "to pay homage to the Grand Master for the time being, and to his Officers when duly installed, and strictly to conform to every Edict of the Grand Lodge". At the time this new oath was introduced the Master Elect risked having his throat cut across if he disobeyed, as the physical penalties of his original Masonic oaths were still in place. In 1813, some twenty seven years after the signing of the US republican constitution and a mere fourteen years after the establishment of republican government in France, this odious edict was introduced as an act of political expediency to ensure support for then unpopular Hanoverian monarchy and stave off a perceived threat of Masonically inspired republicanism taking root in England.

The Worshipful Master of a private lodge is elected by its members to serve their interests. But before he can take his seat in the Chair of King Solomon, to employ and instruct his brethren in Freemasonry, he must first agree that if any conflict of interest arises between the members who elected him and the self-selected central organization which sits in Great Queen Street, he will betray the brethren of his lodge without question. I never cease to be amazed that a constitution which can be so squeamish about the physical penalties as to remove them, against the wishes of the majority of brethren, can keep in place such a public oath of disloyalty to the very brethren who vote to install the Master Elect and pay the costs of UGLE. The original reason for this two hundred year old act of political expediency was to ensure support for then unpopular Hanoverian monarchy and stave off the perceived threat of Masonic led republicanism which had been so successful in the United States of America and in France. I would argue most strongly that the threat of a Masonic republic being set up in England is no longer a major one and that this odious remnant of a frightened and democratically challenged autocratic society could be removed as easily as the physical penalties have already been.

I have consistently refused to take this invidious oath of disloyalty to the brethren of my lodge and so I remain a Master Mason unless, or until, it is removed and consigned to the dustbin of history. Freemasonry's purpose is to develop a Candidate to become a spiritually mature, freethinking, responsible, and silent, past master, who knows himself, is able to think for himself and understands his purpose in this world. While such a restrictive and undemocratic oath remains part of the UGLE Installation ceremony then English Freemasonry is unlikely to revive its fortunes. Remember, the English constitution, under the United Grand Lodge of England, is the only part of the world-wide Masonic fraternity which is so unsure of its democratic authority as to demand such oath.

Now, as Freemasonry's popularity declines back towards what might well be a more natural level of support, unless its hierarchy is reformed to allow the silent office of a past master to become the target achievement of every brother, then perhaps it should be allowed to wither and die. Its patent lack of trust in the loyalty of the Masters of its lodges, makes it unworthy to preserve and pass on what I feel is one of the true spiritual treasures of the western world.

Essay 18- Why become a Freemason?

An Appeal to the Next Generation.

I must admit this is by far the hardest question I have set for myself throughout this whole collection of essays. My reason for asking "Why become a Freemason? is a desire to be solve a personal dilemma. I would like to be able to present a case to younger men to join our Order as I feel it has much of value to pass on, yet I also know it has a great number of shortcomings and dated hierarchical attitudes which can easily drive away the younger, intelligent professionals I would like to see providing fresh blood. I wonder, can Freemasonry still prove an attraction to the next generation's movers and shakers?

The problem may be that Freemasonry deals with questions which are of more concern to older people. At its best it deals with control, restraint and the meaning of life, at its worst it encourages contempt for outside achievement and a desire to exercise ignorant overbearing bullying in the form of snubs and snide put-downs in ways which would never be tolerated in the outside world.

When I try to draw on my own experience I am forced to admit that I continue with Masonry despite many of its grosser features and suppose I will be forced in this essay to try to understand what it is which keeps me attending. I have no trouble defining what I don't like, and it only as I realize just how much of Freemasonry I do dislike that I feel I must attempt to lay out its attractions in a way which I can contribute to the Order's long-term survival.

I recognize that I continue to attend and take part, yet I do not want promotion or even a floor job, which is the normal motive for continuing. Some times I don't find much fellowship within Masonry, a visit to a Science Festival gives me far more fellow feeling with brother scientists and sends me away refreshed and brimming with new ideas. So what is Freemasonry's attraction and how can I explain it to a young, professional in a way which will encourage that individual to join Masonry yet will not so mislead them that they will walk away in disgust when they meet their first big-pinny merchant. Although Freemasonry has good points, its attitude towards young, educated and professional men is totally anachronistic. I am well aware the women's Freemasonry is thriving and growing at as fast a rate as male Freemasonry is declining. Apparently the women have discovered the secret of attracting their younger Sistren whilst we men have not. Is it because they take the teachings of the Masonic Craft more seriously than we males?

My motive for writing this essay is to see if I can put forward a coherent case to the next generation for the survival of Freemasonry.

So why become a Freemason?

What's in it for me then? That would be a typical professional response to the suggestion that you might want to join a a crusty, archaic, self-seeking organization like Freemasonry. What! I'm too young to become a boring old fart yet! But are you?

Let me begin my pitch for your attention by using one word which sums up the benefits and rewards of becoming a Freemason.

That word is Tradition.

Tradition is defined in the Oxford dictionary as

noun 1. the transmission of customs or beliefs from generation to generation.

2. a long-established custom or belief passed on in this way.

3 an artistic or literary method or style established by an artist, writer, or movement, and subsequently followed by others.

You might consider joining Freemasonry so that you can learn something of use to you which has already benefited older generations and could continue to benefit future generations, should you choose to help it continue.

But what does Tradition mean in the context of Freemasonry?

A Tradition of self-help in mastering basic skills.

A Tradition of self-restraint in personal behaviour.

A Tradition of self-improvement as part of a way of becoming a better contributor to society.

Let me add to this a feeling of comradeship which comes from working with kindred spirits on a shared purpose. This is tradition at its best, passing hard -won knowledge from one generation to the next. It is a way to tap into the wisdom and experience of older people who have been interested and motivated enough to wrestle with the most fundamental questions of existence.

But are you the right sort of person to join, does Freemasonry force any of its own demands onto you? How do the requirements of acceptance create a sense of common purpose which makes membership of the The Craft worth pursuing?

Our shared purpose arises from a common philosophical position which is demanded from all candidates from membership. This is expressed as a willingness to affirm a belief that there is some purpose and order at the centre of existence.

One question is put to all prospective new members and this is: "Do you believe in some form of Supreme Being?"

At first sight this question would seem to exclude anyone who does not follow a religious faith, yet in reality the question is deeper than "Do you belong to a Church, Synagogue, Temple or Mosque?" It is really asking do you think that there is some sort of order at the centre of reality, and by implication do you want to know more about it? This question is not necessarily a religious one. Any scientist, no matter in what discipline they work, has to hold a belief that there are basic laws of the cosmos which it is possible to understand and use. Any medical professional believes in the theory of DNA, infection control and the circulation of the blood and so accepts that there are rules which underpin reality. A legal professional has to trust in logic and the process of law which means they have to accept the consistency, and reproducibility, of collective human consciousness.

Having accepted there is a basic order in the universe (what the metaphor of a Supreme Being encapsulates) even if this belief is tinged with the uncertainty which lies at the centre of quantum physics as it does in my case, then Freemasonry offers a way to study this order. It teaches a language of symbol and metaphor which helps put into common words the deep yearnings of the human spirit. It offers comrades who share your interest, it shows you the traditional ways in which previous generations have adapted this knowledge into their lives and how you can bring it into yours and how you can benefit from trying to comprehend the ultimate mysteries of existence.

Freemasonry is the oldest self-help organization in the Western world. It has been helping Masons learn basic skills, such as the art of memory, how to express yourself and how to be confident when speaking in public since the first speculative lodge was recorded in Aberdeen in 1483. Although it is an old established system, which in many ways is crusty and fossilized, it uses techniques such as role-playing, memory work, public speaking, action and double-loop learning which are at the forefront of the teaching methods used in modern universities. Its techniques have evolved to pass on its traditions and its traditions benefit its members by making them better people, more at peace with themselves and the society they live it. Freemasonry creates an environment which enables you to learn about yourself, your fellow lodge members and about society as a whole.

Our first degree teaches you about fear and emotional control. Our second degree encourages you to develop your intellect and power of reasoning. While our third teaches you to face up to the deepest of your night fears and shows you there is hope for the future.

I cannot promise that every lodge can manage to fulfill all the expectations I have raised in this sales pitch, but they are all trying their incompetent best to do so, and if new blood infuses them, new blood keen to learn and preserve the best of their ways, whilst making allowances for some of the historical hierarchical absurdities which still they might occasionally indulge in, then Freemasonry can renew itself and pass its secrets about the human condition on to you and your children for generations to come.

Essay 19 - Some Questions and My Answers

1. Why did I join Masonry?

I had a good opinion of Freemasonry, formed by visiting social occasions at a Women's Lodge (The Lodge of the East Gate, in Chester). I was curious about why Freemasonry seemed to engender good fellowship and a sense of well-being. I was not looking for any sort of spiritual experience. If anything I was only looking for social contact. What I found surprised me.

2. What surprised me about Masonry when I first joined?

Make no mistake about it, Freemasonry is odd when you first encounter it. Think back to how it first appeared to you as a Candidate. Try to view it with the eyes of a child, not with the familiarity you have built up over many years of repetition.

When I was interviewed by a panel of past masters what I was joining was virtually unknown. The only firm question that had been put to me was "Do you believe in a Supreme Being?". I did, because as a physicist I was totally committed to the idea that there are laws which govern the whole of the cosmos. Everything proceeded from there to the point where I was stood with an armed guard who was banging with the hilt of a sword on the large door to the temple, seeking permission for me to enter.

I was blindfolded and strangely dressed in loose fitting white trousers and top. Unbeknown to me a hangman's noose had been put around my neck and draped down my back. All metal objects had been taken from me and I was now ready to be led into the Temple. (I later learned that this mode of dress, the rough smock with the running noose about the neck, was exactly how a medieval heretic would have been treated by the Inquisition prior to making a final confession).

As I entered the temple I sensed a large number of people present and felt totally vulnerable. A cold point pressed on the skin of my chest.

"Do you feel anything?" the voice in front asked. A whisper in my ear gave the formalized reply which I repeated out aloud. "I do".

"Then let this be a sting to your conscience as well as instant death should you ever betray any of the secrets now about to be imparted to you."

Another voice from the other side of the room then spoke - "As no man can be made a Mason unless he be free and of mature age, I now demand of you- are you a free man and of the full age of twenty one years?"

Again I was told what to say and I repeated

"I am".

"Having answered that question so satisfactorily, there are others which I shall immediately proceed to put to you which I trust you will answer with equal candour. Do you seriously declare on your honour that, unbiased by the improper solicitations of friends against your own inclinations, uninfluenced by mercenary or any other unworthy motive, you freely and voluntarily offer yourself as a candidate for the mysteries and privileges of Freemasonry? Do you further seriously declare on your honour that you are prompted to solicit these privileges from a favourable opinion preconceived of our Order, a general desire for knowledge and a sincere wish to render yourself more extensively serviceable to your fellow creatures?"

I would have had no trouble in saying "yes" to this question, but I was instructed to say.

"I do."

The sword point that had been held to my chest was taken away but the noose remained around my neck. The man at my right hand whispered for me to kneel and a short prayer was said, invoking the blessing of the Great Architect of the Universe.

The ceremony proceeded with my helper guiding me around the perimeter of the temple pausing, three times to introduce me as a *poor candidate in a state of darkness`*.

After stumbling round for what seemed a long period of time I was told to stand still while somebody asked me.

"Having been in a state of darkness for so long, what is the predominant wish of your heart?"

Again I was not left to answer for myself but told what to say.

"Light".

The blindfold was removed from behind and as my eyes adjusted I heard the sound of a muffled clapping.

The Worshipful Master then showed me the emblematic `lights` of Freemasonry, which were explained as being the Volume of the Sacred Law, the Square and the Compasses. He told me that I had now attained the rank of Entered Apprentice Freemason- the first of three degrees through which I would have to pass before being accepted as a full Master Mason. The secret signs, grips and password of the first degree were then explained to me and I was told that the left hand pillar that stood in the porchway of King Solomon's Temple has special significance. Both the left-hand and right-hand pillars were recreated in the lodge and stood behind, and to either side of the Master. I was reminded that the left hand pillar is called Boaz, and it was named after Boaz, the great-grandfather of David, King of Israel.

After various perambulations around the Temple I was presented with a simple white calf skin apron which symbolized the rank I had just obtained. Then I was told. "It is more ancient than the Golden Fleece or Roman Eagle, more honourable than the

Star, Garter or any other order now in existence, it being the badge of innocence and the bond of friendship."

Throughout the course of the ceremony various moral and social virtues were recommended to me using a number of architectural analogies; stonemason's tools were likened to methods of self-improvement. Towards the end of the ceremony of initiation, I was alarmed to learn that there are test questions which I had to commit to memory before I could progress to the next degree. Amongst these questions and answers were some pieces of information that were more intriguing than informing:

Question. "What is Freemasonry?"

Answer. "A peculiar system of morality, veiled in allegory and illustrated by symbols."

Question. "What are the three grand principles upon which Freemasonry is founded?"

Answer. "Brotherly love, relief and truth."

To any candidate the first of these principles sounds reasonable but the next two are a little hard to fathom. Relief from what? Which truth?

I left the temple that night feeling that something special had happened; but I didn't have a clue as to what any of it might mean. Perhaps, I thought, all will become clear at the next ceremony.

It did not. Even now, many years later it has still not become completely clear.

There is little of the Masonic ritual that could be described as ordinary. The Candidate is blindfolded, stripped of money and metal objects, dressed as an accused heretic on his journey to the gallows and finally told that the object of his last degree is 'how to die'. The journey from darkness to light is obviously important as are the two pillars called Boaz and Jachin that symbolise 'strength' and 'establishment' and when united, mean 'stability'.

Freemasonry claims to be more ancient than the Golden Fleece or Roman Eagle and has the aim of brotherly love, relief and truth - yet investigating the hidden mysteries of nature and science are presented as very important. The genuine secrets of the Order, I was told, are lost and substituted secrets are in their place until such time as the true ones will be found.

The central character of Freemasonry is the builder of King Solomon's Temple who is named as Hiram Abif, and who was murdered by three of his own men. A re-enactment of his stylized death is the act that made me a Master Mason and when I was raised from my temporary tomb, the bright hopeful light of the morning star rose on the horizon of the lodge.

At the time I wondered where could such strange ideas have developed, and why? And what are the rituals trying to teach? These are questions I have been worrying away at ever since. I have since written many books about this strange craft but each time I arrive at answers I find I have uncovered even more questions. So my quest to understand more and more remains fresh.

3. What do I think Freemasonry has achieved?

Freemasonry has been an engine of achievement that drove the world from darkness to light.

Its members were the great and the good, the people who ran the Church, the country, industry, the armed forces and academia. They were the entrepreneurs and the intelligentsia who made the industrial revolution and who pioneered social and scientific advancement.

Europe thrived on it and the British Empire spread the Order to every corner of the planet. The oldest universities such as Oxford and Cambridge were proud of their lodges, the great ship builders and the men who took the American railroads westwards mingled with the judges and the generals to work together for a better society. Ambition was in their bellies and achievement was their only acceptable outcome.

The American Constitution and the Royal Society came into existence because of Masons like George Washington, Benjamin Franklin, Sir Robert Moray, Alexander Bruce and Elias Ashmole.

The city of Washington was designed by Freemasons and London raised from the ashes of the Great Fire due to the inspiration of Grand Master Mason, Sir Christopher Wren. Even the 'Wild West' was tamed by Freemasons Davy Crockett, Jim Bowie, Buffalo Bill and Pat Garatt to name but a few.

In every town throughout the western world Masonic temples provided the meeting ground for the men who set out to achieve. In the town in West Yorkshire town of Halifax where I choose to live, the world's largest building society was brought into existence by Freemasons who met in the Old Cock Inn. This institution, named after the town, provided the financial structure to give hundreds of thousands of ordinary people the new opportunity to own their own home.

At a time when leading thinkers and doers were either Christians or Jews, Freemasons of all religions met on equal terms in the lodge to share their enthusiasm for progress on the road to making life better for themselves, their families and the community at large. They worked in harmony with their church or synagogue as any religious differences evaporated in the atmosphere of tolerance that is central to the Order.

As they achieved ever greater success their towns and their countries grew more prosperous and new, more specialist, ways of working together came along. Freemasonry fought for and attained an age of reason and personal freedom. It encouraged people to develop themselves and their communities in in doing so reduced the need for seekers after truth to meet in darkened rooms, wear strange regalia and recite odd-ball ritual. The end result is that no longer are the majority of Masonic lodges the meeting place of 'movers and shakers'.

The people who would once have been the backbone of the Order, now would not dream of asking to join. They think they have better things to do in their life; careers to build, families to rear and a wide variety of social commitments to take up their time. Everyone from businessmen to police officers, from councillors to academics give the order a wide berth. These days membership of the local lodge can be seen as either irrelevant or positively detrimental to a young person's career. It was not always this way, and the teachings of Freemasonry which brought about these social changes are still there to inspire further generations, if they choose to learn.

4. What does Freemasonry have to offer in the modern world?

I believe that Masonry is an ancient system which seeks to improve the mental and spiritual condition of its followers. It can be understood and it can be explained. Its secrets, however, cannot be given away. They can only be experienced and understood by enacting and internalizing them. That is why we practice ritual.

I believe there is a philosophy which underlies Freemasonry and which indicates how its teachings can be used as a way to develop your own spirit.

Over the years I have made a detailed study of the rituals of Freemasonry. From this I have come to the conclusion that they show a depth of understanding that is not widely known, but offers a way to spiritual growth. Whilst Freemasonry is not a religion itself, it is spiritual technique that is compatible with the belief systems of any religion, and also with the rational world-view of science. Within its teachings it has the potential to provide a focal point for many people who are not active in any particular faith – and for them it might be a replacement for religion because it provides spiritual values without a need to subscribe to an entire belief system. It is tolerant in a way that most religions are not and its symbolic teaching allows a range of interpretation that enfolds people of all beliefs allowing them to take what they need from its system. In this way they can learn more about themselves and the needs of their spirit. To share in these secrets all they need is an acceptance that there is order underpinning the behaviour of the universe, to be able say yes, they believe in a Supreme Being or at least a Supreme Giver of Order.

It is my belief that Freemasonry is an ancient science that has shaped human ambition, achievement and well-being. It may yet offer greater insights into the mystery of the inner self, that will enhance rather than conflict with modern science. But if it is to do so, we must learn to understand what it is and how our generation may best teach it to our successors.

Endnotes

1 Quoted in Jammer (1999), p. 47.

2 Quoted in Jammer (1999), p. 48.

3 Heisenberg (1958), p. 135.

4 Schrödinger (1967), pp. 138–9

5 Quoted in Farmelo (2010) pp 376-377

6 Feynman (1988), pp. 243–4.

7 Hoyle (1983), pp. 243–4.

8 Hawking, S.W. (1985), Letter to the Editors, *American Scientist*, vol. 73, no. 12.

9 Hoyle (1983), pp. 248–9.

10 Jung, CG. *Man and his Symbols.* London: Aldus, 1964.

11 Phaedo 75b

12 http://www-history.mcs.st-andrews.ac.uk/Biographies/Wallis.html

13 http://www.isaacnewton.ca/gen_scholium/scholium.htm

14 http://202.38.126.65/navigate/math/history/Mathematicians/Wallis.html

15 http://www.newton.ac.uk/newtlife.html

16 http://www.maths.tcd.ie/pub/HistMath/People/Newton/RouseBall/RB_Newton.html

17

http://www.maths.tcd.ie/pub/HistMath/People/Newton/RouseBall/RB
_Newton.html

18 Rouse Ball, W.W. *A Short Account of the History of Mathematics.*
New York: Dover Press, 1908.

19 Penrose, R. *The Road to Reality. 2004.*

20 See DeGroot, 2004.

21 See Zimmerman, 1996.

22 See DeGroot, 2004.

23 Hoyle (1983), pp. 198–9.

Bibliography

Dirac P. (1930), *The Principles of Quantum Mechanics*, Clarendon Press, London (4th edition 1981).

DeGroot, Gerard (2004) *The Bomb: A life*, Jonathan Cape, London .

Farmelo, G. (2010), *The Strangest Man*, Faber, London.

Feynman, R.P. (1985), *QED: The Strange Theory of Light and Matter*, Princeton University Press, Princeton NJ.

— — (1988), *What Do You Care What Other People Think?* Unwin, London.

Hawking, S.W. (1985), Letter to the Editors, *American Scientist*, vol. 73, no. 12.

Heisenberg, W. (1958), *Physics and Philosophy*, Penguin, London

Hoyle, F. (1983), *The Intelligent Universe*, Michael Joseph, London.

Jammer, M. (1999), *Einstein and Religion*, Princeton University Press, Princeton NJ.

Jung, CG. (1964) *Man and his Symbols.*: Aldus,. London

Penrose, R. (2004), *The Road to Reality*, BCA, London

Rouse Ball, W.W. (1908) *A Short Account of the History of Mathematics.* Dover Press, New York

Schrödinger, E. (1967), *What is Life?* Cambridge University Press, Cambridge.

Zimmerman, David (1996) *Top Secret Exchange: The Tizard mission and the scientific war,* McGill-Queen's University Press, Montreal..